Three "books" in one, Noel Tyl's *Special Horoscope Dimensions: Success, Sex and Illness* provides a thorough introduction to vocational and medical Astrology, plus an area often neglected, the sexual profile in the horoscope.

The vocational section deals with the Moon in the Houses, the oriental planet, elemental and modal emphasis, the Jupiter-Saturn alliance. Practically, it treats vocational guidance and relocation. Its treatment of vocational guidance avoids the overschematic approach typical of the field, following instead Tyl's "law of naturalness." Vocational guidance is viewed as the fruition of whole-life analysis, just as work is a natural extension of the whole identity.

The section on sex is remarkably thorough, covering the sexual profile in the horoscope in terms of planetary significators, retrogradation, hemisphere emphasis, planet-sign and aspect signification. Specialized topics such as homosexuality and trans-sexualism are covered, but the focus is primarily on the ability or inability emotionally and sexually to *share* in a relationship. Special fields covered are synastry (chart comparison) and determination of the fertility cycle and the sex of the unborn child.

The approach to medical Astrology is unique in its emphasis on illness as a predisposition pervading the organic system, which is triggered by an imbalance in need fulfillment. Medical symbolism, including reflex and sympathetic action, is covered in detail, as are topics such as vitality, hypochondria, nutrition, and death.

Throughout, the discussion of these far-ranging topics is illuminated by 49 detailed charts. Synastry is explained, for example, through a brilliant analysis of the relationship of Eva Braun and Adolph Hitler; hypochondria, through the chart of Howard Hughes; the finer points of vocational astrology as an extension of whole-life analysis, through Patricia Hearst's chart.

These three "books," despite their thoroughness, are fused together by the author's concern with relationships as the focus of life. Work ties the individual to society; sex and love, to other individuals; and illness is often a malfunction of relationships in these two areas.

SPECIAL HOROSCOPE DIMENSIONS

Volume IX

The Principles and Practice of Astrology

The Llewellyn Syllabus
for home study and college curriculum

The Principles and Practice
of Astrology

NOEL TYL

A complete text for instruction and reference in the practice of
standard astrological methods and the psychological and
philosophical principles for analysis and application. In 12 volumes.

Volume IX

SPECIAL HOROSCOPE DIMENSIONS
Sex, Success and Illness

1975
Llewellyn Publications
Saint Paul, Minnesota, 55165, U.S.A.

First Edition 1975

Llewellyn Publications
Post Office Box 3383
Saint Paul, Minnesota 55165

International Standard Book Number: 0-87542-808-8
Library of Congress Catalog Card Number: 73-19924

Printed in the United States of America

There are two ways of spreading light:
to be the candle
or the mirror that reflects it.

Edith Wharton

Contents

Introduction

By their works are men and women known. Enterprising participation with the environment, human and material, establishes man's identity within life development. Work satisfies many needs. In many ways, life is a job. "What do you do for a living?" is an extremely significant question.

Man and woman were created "to be fruitful, to multiply and fill the Earth." Our fundamental sexual polarity reflects day and night, creation within the flow of time. Creativity is the primal energy. It is the essence of self-esteem, the energy of relationships, the essential purpose of life. It is the living force.

Illness keeps men and women from doing work, from improving relationships. It reflects a break in the flow of essential energies. It is a symptom of frustration, mental and physical. Illness interrupts man's purpose.

The horoscope portrays success, sex, and illness in its delineation of identity within a challenging environment. Peace with respect to these special horoscope dimensions promises efficiency and fulfillment in the art of living.

1

1

Success

Even more than through religion, the world population is organized and stratified through individual work effort. Labor unions become political forces. Sociology is fundamentally based upon an individual's job. Through his work, man makes money, creates an external identity, forms relationships, fills time, and sometimes gains a place in history. To a great extent, "What do you do for a living?" means "What kind of person are you?"

In relationships, our reactions are initially based upon a person's method of earning a living. Social groups are formed on the basis of the job, the income level that almost always reflects the job status. Definition of a person's work presupposes a specific level of education, an expected life style, a defined significance within the sociological scheme of things.

The individual is in the very center. Bureaucracy frames what he or she does to live. The job determines self-esteem, fulfillment of intrinsic inclination, growth within the real world. The job gives the individual identity

3

in relationship to others. The person becomes a title, a number, a function; a specialist; a leader, servant; a doer, thinker, reactor. One uses one's head, energy, and creativity to find "a place in the Sun"; man expresses individuality through personal ambition; he hopes for recognition and reward.

Perhaps the most popular questions received by an astrologer from a client are "What job should I be in?", "What work can I do best?", and "What direction should I follow, what should I do with my life?" These questions ask for vocational guidance through Astrology. An individual's happiness and feeling of success are dependent to a very great degree upon finding the right direction, the most suitable job—and doing it well.

Philosophically and psychologically, we can take this premise one step further: individuals perform best when they are doing *what they need to do*. This is when they are at one with themselves and their place within nature and the material and human environments. This unity releases the efficiency that leads to self-fulfillment; identity is defined and secured; individual life has direction, function, and significance.

In this sense, "success" is not simply a subjective feeling or an objective evaluation. The concept of success is above all a gestalt of self-fulfillment in terms of individual needs. It is the outcome of horoscope *deployment*, the full use of individualistic astrological potentials.

In Volume V (*Astrology and Personality*), need theory was studied intensively. The Moon was suggested as a symbol of the personality's form in terms of reigning needs to be fulfilled throughout the process of becoming. The aspects to the Moon were viewed as the environmental "press" upon the major needs, the tension that challenges behavior to fulfill needs. In the study of vocational guidance and the goal of success in life, the Moon again is the key. It reflects our position in world experience by House position, our expression of psychological needs through Sign tenancy, and the tensions toward fulfillment through aspect patterns.

The Moon in the Houses

When the Moon is within the Ascendant, the emphasis is upon individuality, "doing your own thing." The attitude within work toward success is highly individualized. Harry Truman, with the Moon in the Ist in Scorpio, is a perfect example; also Lyndon Johnson, George Bernard Shaw, Theodore Roosevelt, Nelson Rockefeller. This position of the Moon symbolizes individualistic personal internalization of environmental influences. There is a personal interpretation given to all experience. Reactions are highly individualized. Mood fluctuation is pronounced. The unique appeals more than the routine. (*Of course, House placement is conditioned by the psychological needs represented by the Moon in its Sign; modified through the Moon's aspect network.*)

When the Moon is within the IInd House, the reflected light of the Sun emphasizes self-worth. The individual needs a work structure that allows public view and evaluation. Like a shiny object within a display case, the individual with the Moon in the IInd should be on public view while working. This does not necessarily mean working with the public (House VII) directly; the emphasis is upon being seen while working (as opposed to not being seen at all when the Moon is in the XIIth). Examples: Zsa Zsa Gabor, Leonard Bernstein, Joan Baez, Julie Andrews, Patricia Hearst.

The Moon in the IIIrd House emphasizes the communication and exchange dimensions within work toward success. The personality gathers, shares, and reacts to information. The Moon in the IIIrd represents the intermediary, the go-between, the dissemination functions: Thomas Edison, Adolf Hitler, Jack London, Prince Philip, Johnny Carson.

When the Moon is in the IVth House, the House of its natural rulership, the home is highly emphasized within the work situation. Often, this Moon position suggests that the person would be most fulfilled working from within the home; or the person makes his or her place of work very homey, using photographs, furniture, etc., to establish the most comfortable atmosphere. The need during work is for security and comfort that most often are symbolized by the home. Additionally, within a strongly spiritual horoscope, the dimension of the soul can be very important. Examples are Franz Liszt, Truman Capote, Madame Helena Blavatsky, Carl Sandburg, Pablo Picasso, Howard Hughes.

The Vth House position of the Moon increases the theatrical, exhibitionistic, creative dimensions of the work needs. Teaching and care of children are also emphasized.

There can be the appeal of speculation, the dramatizing of all experiences. Examples: the boxer Muhammed Ali, Amelia Earhart, Douglas Fairbanks, Billy Graham, Ernest Hemingway, Bob Hope, Laurence Olivier, Jacqueline Onassis.

When the Moon is in the VIth House, the individual is usually totally absorbed within the work situation. He or she can be a "workaholic." Work is easily all-consuming. Yet, the Moon in the VIth suggests that there will be many job changes, searching for the ideal position, and/or great versatility. Examples are Benjamin Franklin, Albert Einstein, Richard Nixon, Lucille Ball, John F. Kennedy, Jr.

As the first half of the horoscope House system is completed, a pattern within quadrants is discovered: when the Moon is in an Angle, the manifestation of the symbolism is highly active, energized; the individual imposes himself upon the work situation. When the Moon is in a Succedent House, the symbolism suggests a particular kind of organization within the work structure. In a Cadent House, the symbolism shows a reaction function to work situations, suggests a response profile that determines one's function and contentment within work. This pattern holds throughout the second half of the horoscope as well, with the dimension of "others" more highly emphasized.

When the Moon is in the VIIth, of course, the work situation is tied to public reflection, partnerships, a keen awareness of public expectation and the need to meet it. Perhaps marriage is essential to give clear focus to work security. In the majority of cases, the work profile can be labeled a "public personality." The individual is dependent upon others for the fulfillment of work needs. The process of relationships is extremely important. Examples are Dwight Eisenhower, John D. Rockefeller, Jr., Marilyn Monroe, Dean Martin.

The VIIIth House Moon suggests a work situation dependent upon others' resources, a comfort within another's organization, a fulfillment through reconstruction, possibly reform. There is the appeal of rehabilitation. Additionally, there can be dimensions of mystery, research, religion, and sexuality within the work profile. Remember, when the Moon is within the VIIIth, the *personality* factors within character analysis are often not easily accessible; there can be the registration of aloofness. In the specific dimension of work preference, it is a logical extension of the personality to be deployed *indirectly*, within and through the organization of and by others, to seek the self through reorganization within the works of others, or supported by others. Examples: Louis Pasteur, Nikita Khruschchev, General George Patton, Alfred Hitchcock, Ted Kennedy.

When the Moon is in the IXth, a Cadent House, the emphasis is placed upon higher mind reactions, the dimensions of philosophy, public mores, sharing the reasoning of the public. There is a premium placed upon vicarious fulfillment. Individuality loses significance. Additionally, the dimensions of foreign travel, relocation, even citizenship change are important dimensions to consider in the quest for work conditions that will bring personal success. Examples: Martin Luther, Voltaire, George Washington, Edgar Cayce.

When the Moon is placed within the Midheaven, the Xth, it can be the most elevated body within the whole horoscope. This angular Moon represents a "take charge" energy within work situations. It is an authoritarian power position. The individuality is emphasized, often to the point that no subordinate position within work can be easily tolerated. The Moon is in the Xth in the horoscope of the United States, Franklin D. Roosevelt, Thomas Jefferson, Harry Houdini, John Dillinger, Charles Manson, Robert Kennedy, Steve McQueen.

In the XIth House, the Moon symbolism emphasizes the network of friendships within the work situation. Friends help get the job, make the job rewarding, and endure after the job is left. The advice of a friend, the friend's speculation about work opportunity, direction, or evaluation is often more important than that of professional counsellors, agencies, or work leaders. Examples: Princess Anne of England, Ingrid Bergman, John F. Kennedy.

When the Moon is in the XIIth House, the individual prefers little or no contact at all with the public within the job situation. Symbolically, this position is the author hidden away in the attic, the playwright who will not attend a performance of his work, the behind-the-scenes person. Again, we must remember that, characterologically, having the Moon in the XIIth somehow hides the personality, can limit and confine it. In work, these conditions are preferred to provide maximum comfort to the personality. Examples: Abraham Lincoln, Fred Astaire, Greta Garbo, Bob Dylan, Marlene Dietrich, Pope Paul VI.

The Oriental Planet

The Moon in the Houses provides a major indication of the experience focus, conditions, and reactions of the work needs. Analysis begins with this dimension and is augmented by the significance of the Sun-Moon Sign blend (Volume III), the House placement of the Sun, and the Sign upon the Ascendant. The beginnings of character analysis are focused upon analysis of work need, the fulfillment of which will bring success to the identity.

Study of the Ascendant introduces another very simple and very productive measurement: the first planet that will rise (clockwise motion) over the Ascendant immediately before the Sun, i.e., the planet next *behind* the Sun in longitude placement within the horoscope, regardless of the separation between them, provides another key to the type of vocation that will help to fulfill the individual. The planet rising just before the Sun is called the "oriental" (eastward) planet.

If Mercury is oriental, the individual will be oriented toward routine work, detail, direct cooperation with what's demanded in any situation. There's the possibility of a need to conform, to find work security within repetition, to gain satisfaction simply (Adlai Stevenson, Dwight Eisenhower).

If Venus is oriental, attention to ego, an awareness of style within work are very important. The person adopts the work function as his or her very own. The work belongs to the person or is dependent upon the personality for objective evaluation (Franklin D. Roosevelt, Barbara Streisand, Joan Sutherland).

Mars oriental suggests the promoter, the person who can toot the horn in favor of the work situation. Dedication is strong, the sense of advertising is energetic (P.T. Barnum, Janis Joplin, Shelley Winters, Lyndon Johnson, Johnny Carson, Evel Knievel).

Jupiter oriental symbolizes the person who will take the easy way within all work situations. Getting things done quickly pleases. Enthusiasm comes in large doses but threatens to disappear throughout a long effort (John F. Kennedy, Richard Nixon, the U.S.A.).

Saturn oriental symbolizes patience, plodding stick-to-itiveness, the long haul, mature perspectives within work aspiration (Woodrow Wilson, Martin Luther King, Ralph Nader).

When Uranus rises just before the Sun, anything that is dangerous, adventurous, or innovative will have the highest work appeal. The work effort may be an outlet for nervousness. Diversity will appeal (El Cordobes, Rasputin, Charles de Gaulle, Joe Namath).

When Neptune is oriental, the search for perfection leads the pursuit for work success. Dreams and visionary planning are important dimensions of the job hunt and work organization. The hope is for harmony between what is expected and what can be. (Nelson Rockefeller, Julie Andrews).

When Pluto is oriental, the dimension of personal

perspective is very important. The personality is attracted to the opportunities to gain personal prominence and power through the work situation (Sigmund Freud, Neil Armstrong, Merv Griffin).

If the Moon itself is oriental, the last body to rise before the Sun, the collective ideal of the people is most important. It is the position of the team coach, the teacher, the manager, perhaps the prophet (Harry S. Truman, Frank Lloyd Wright, George Wallace, Pope Paul VI).

Basic Analysis

With just the Moon in its House and Sign, blended with the Sun and the Ascendant, and recognition of the oriental planet, vocational analysis of the horoscope is well under way. This analysis delineates the identity's intrinsic work inclinations. Fulfilling these inclinations within time, in terms of the tension factors placed upon them by the full personality and its interaction with the environment, provides the individual's measure of personal achievement and success. Let's look at some partial horoscopes and see how much can be told vocationally from them.

In example 1 the Moon is in the IXth House, ruling Cancer on the IXth. This man's vocational need is linked to philosophical reactions of the higher mind. The Sun-Moon blend (Volume III) suggests the noble romantic, a social idealism expressed dramatically or artistically. The Scorpio Ascendant suggests the personal involvement with mystery, primal concerns, research, the significance of emotions and spirituality. Saturn rises last before the Sun and is in conjunction with the Moon: an enormous patience in the search for wisdom. Saturn rules the IIIrd and IVth, suggesting the communication objective of all the acquired knowledge. This is a part of the horoscope of Marc Edmund Jones (1 October 1888; 8:37 A.M. CST, St. Louis), perhaps the finest astrological thinker, researcher, and innovator in the history of the United States. His many books are in great demand, and his lectures still stimulate and enrich students and professionals. In his own listing of his birth data, Dr. Jones (psychology, the ministry) lists himself as "an occultist."

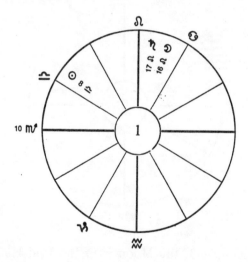

In example 2 the Moon is in the IIIrd House: the work need will be to communicate, to exchange information, to act as a go-between. This is strongly emphasized by the fact that the Moon is in Gemini. The

Sun-Moon blend suggests the dangers of instability through indecision that must be overcome through concentration and planning. The Aries Ascendant shows a projected image of leadership, wanting to be the first, the most important. Jupiter oriental again shows a dangerous tendency toward flightiness, an over-inflation of self-importance perhaps, in terms of philosophy, ethics, and internationalism. This is a part of the horoscope of the United Nations whose charter was signed on 24 October 1945, 4:45 P.M., EST, in Washington, D.C.

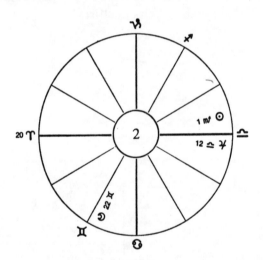

In example 3, the Moon is in the IInd House: this woman needs to become one with her work, to identify personally with a life mission perhaps, and to project this within a public structure. The evaluation of work success is the same as an evaluation of her self. She needs exposure to gain success. With the Moon in Libra, these social awareness dimensions are emphasized greatly. The Sun-Moon blend promises a grand exposure of the emotions to society, an adaptation of "social situations to temperamental needs. There may be a curious repression when society turns things around and demands that the Self's emotional needs adapt to those of others" (Volume III). Mars is oriental, suggesting the promotional element within the work need to bring fulfillment to the personality. With Mars in Sagittarius and angular, the projection of ideas, philosophy, ethics is very strong. The

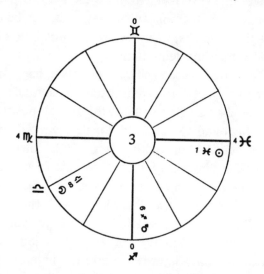

advertising energy would be vast. This is part of the horoscope of Patricia Hearst (20 February 1954; 6:01 P.M., PST, San Francisco), who was presumed kidnapped and then emerged as the symbolic propaganda leader of the Symbionese Liberation Army, focusing her criticisms of society upon her publisher father (Mars in Sagittarius in IV, square the Sun).

Refinements

After the basic work needs are determined and the core energy blend of the Sun, Moon, and Ascendant are adjusted in suggested meaning to focus upon vocation, keyed by the oriental planet; refinements must be added to the deductions in order to establish reference to specific work possibilities. Refinement measurements begin with the Xth House, its ruler and the planets that may be placed there and their aspects; then the whole horoscope is keyed through accumulating deductions.

In the United Nations chart (example 2, page 14), the Midheaven is Capricorn—administration—and its ruler, Saturn, is at 24 Cancer in the IVth, a weak position for Saturn by Sign and House. Additionally, this Saturn is in very close conjunction with Mars (46'), ruler of the Ascendant. The angularity (IVth) of this focus suggests easily that the function of the organization as we know it through the Moon's House, Sign, blend with the Sun, the Ascendant, and the oriental Jupiter is to administer powerfully, but the function of administration can run "hot and cold" (Mars-Saturn); caution and impulse will vie for ascendancy. Perhaps there will be too much concern for *internal* security of the organization (Cancer), keeping it together, and not enough for fulfilling the world administrative function (Capricorn). Perhaps external administration operations bog down in internal insecurity.

Patricia Hearst (full chart on page 18) has a Gemini Midheaven with Jupiter in Gemini in the Xth. Mercury is retrograde in Pisces in the VIIth. The retrogradation of the Midheaven ruler suggests strongly the counterpoint in her choice of work, vocation, profession. "Something else" needs to be said through the personal effort, through self-application. The duality of the Midheaven Sign echoes this deduction. Either more than one work outlet will be pursued or more than one motive or need will be followed. Mercury is exactly square the Midheaven Jupiter, dispositor of the oriental Mars in Sagittarius in the IVth (the home, the publisher father). This square between Mercury and Jupiter promises that exaggeration will hinder judgment, that Patricia will stick to her guns though her ammunition is gone. These considerations are all-important here since Jupiter is co-ruler of the Sun's Sign and Mercury rules the hypercritical Virgo Ascendant. At the time of her kidnapping, natal Mars had progressed to exact opposition to Jupiter and square to Mercury.

The consideration of these dimensions of work need and fulfillment energies so easily involves the whole horoscope. Patricia Hearst's full horoscope immediately brings the whole picture into focus, based upon the parts already analyzed.

The XIIth House Pluto, dispositor of Saturn, suggests that she is frustrated with the world for not understanding her (Volume II). Saturn in Scorpio would symbolize her ambition as complex and self-defensive, responsive only through a cloak of secrecy or through extremely self-regenerating introspection. Additionally, Saturn is

Patricia Hearst
February 20, 1954; 6:01 PST
San Francisco; 37 N 47—122 W 26

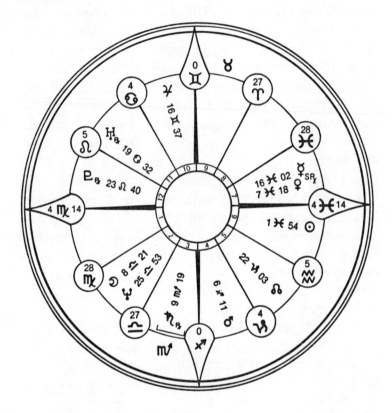

retrograde, suggesting that her father perhaps did not give her the encouragement or discipline she needed in earlier life, or that she feels that he did not. Mutable Signs on the Angles dominating the chart show her malleability, her tendency to over-reaction, her vulnerability to outside influences.

There is no doubt that Patricia Hearst had a large reservoir of energy accumulated through her personal frustrations which drove her to break away from the norm. In any case, she would definitely have become some kind of publicist, writer, social critic, social martyr, working for a complicated ideal that she felt was embodied within her (Water Grand Trine: Venus-Mercury, Uranus, Saturn). Mars is so very powerful here: angular and square the Sun, the Ascendant, and Venus, which is dispositor of the Moon and ruler of the communications IIIrd.

The next example, page 20, has the Moon in the VIIIth: the native's work would be closely involved with others. He would reconstruct or reorganize. With the Moon opposing Pluto, his work need would be to establish or change perspective (Pluto rules VI, actual work and service conditions). The Sun in Aquarius in the Midheaven and the Moon in Capricorn would suggest a powerful administrative leadership ability. He's the rugged, individualistic campaigner who sways the crowd. This is reinforced by the strong squares between the Moon and Jupiter and Uranus, ruler of the Midheaven; by Saturn's prominence in the Midheaven as well.

Saturn is oriental: he'd be patient, hard-driving; he'd stick to it. He would work alone, on his own somehow

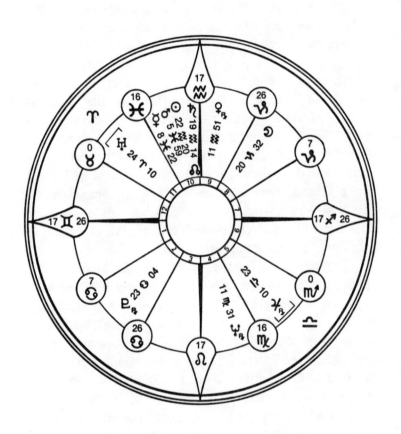

within others' structures (Sun-Saturn conjunction; Moon ruling Cancer on II from within the opposition with Pluto). All these deductions tell us that he is a free-lancer cooperating with and dependent upon others.

What does he do, what fills out these contours of work need? Mercury rules the Ascendant (communication). The Moon rules Cancer also on III (communication). He's a free-lance communicator; strong, persuasive, flexible; he's got unique ideas which he uses to reconstruct other peoples', other companies' perspectives. These ideas are creative in detail (Mercury rules Virgo on V; Jupiter in Libra in V is square with the Moon and opposes Uranus, ruler of the Midheaven and dispositor of Venus, Saturn and Sun). Mercury is dispositor of Neptune, which is in opposition with Mercury in the professional axis. And also, they are in mutual reception! Venus, dispositor of Jupiter in the Vth, is in exact quincunx with Neptune.

All planets below the horizon are retrograde. The man throws himself into experiences strongly, swaying the crowd, winning them with his individuality, creativity, and personal perspectives. There simply is no doubt about it: this man needs to be a free-lance artist.

What kind of art work would he do, what would be the artistic style that would express him best? Mercury is the key as ruler of the Ascendant, the Vth, and in opposition and mutual reception with Neptune within the professional axis. His work would be highly detailed, he would use a tiny brush or a very sharp pencil, requiring lots of patience. Where would such careful drawing be

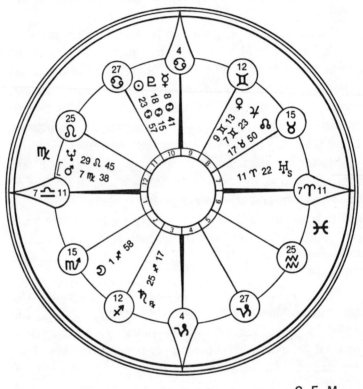

C F M
7 1 6
F A W E
5 3 5 1

most at a premium within business? Fashion design perhaps, catalogue drawings. The native has been the head of the art departments of several extremely well-known department stores. His specialty is catalogue art, with the finest of details in every drawing. His ideas for new styles of catalogue presentation have earned him great success.

The woman in the next example, page 22, has the Moon in the IInd. She will need to be in public view, identified personally somehow with what she does. This deduction is reinforced by the Moon's rulership of the professional Midheaven and disposing of Mercury, Pluto, and the Sun; by the fact that Pluto is oriental; by Uranus stationary in the public VII, square the Xth House group, ruling Aquarius on the VIth; by the Mars position in XII, associated with "bucking the organization."

The Sun-Moon blend suggests that her work needs involve aspiring to very lofty goals, that the beautiful, the aesthetic, the ethical and philosophical will all have great attraction (Volume III). We begin to sense the professional classical artist.

The Libra Ascendant is ruled by Venus in conjunction with Jupiter (dispositor of the Moon) in Gemini (artistic communication through others), and this conjunction is squared by Mars. The aesthetic communication is given great developmental tension. (Mars is dispositor of Uranus and rules the VIIth; Mercury disposes of Mars and is placed at the Midheaven).

Saturn (ambition) in Sagittarius in the IIIrd would express a strong desire to communicate great aesthetic ideas, perhaps in foreign lands.

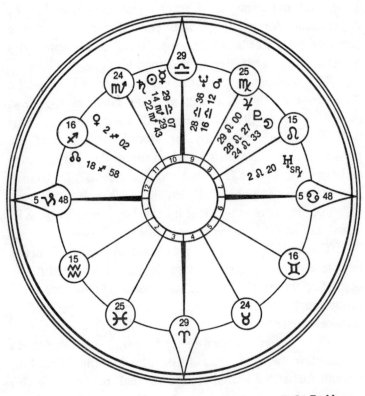

```
      C F M
      5 8 1
      F A W E
      6 4 3 1
```

There's no doubt that we are seeing the chart of a highly specialized, highly individualized public artist, a woman of precise technique (Mars in Virgo). She is an internationally celebrated prima ballerina.

The horoscope on page 24 shows a complete emphasis of the southern hemisphere: the young girl (eighteen) is surely swept away, victimized by experiences. Her Moon in the VIIIth shows her involvement with other peoples' resources. Mercury is oriental, suggesting a routinized compliance with what's expected of her. The Sun-Moon blend suggests that the emotional dimension will run away with the personality. Mercury and Neptune are in exact conjunction with the Midheaven: a music reference but also a potential for self-delusion. Saturn and the Sun in Scorpio and angular introduce the sexual dimension; the Moon-Pluto-Jupiter conjunction in Leo suggests a theatrical dimension.

The only supportive aspect within the whole horoscope is the very close trine between Venus and Uranus. This is very important since Venus rules the Midheaven and the creative Vth (sex, theatricality, speculation) and Uranus rules Aquarius on the IInd, income, self-worth. Uranus is in the public and/or husband's House ruled by the Moon.

The horoscope is confusing and vague, but the possibilities are clear: the young girl would be aspiring to a musical career and/or be a prostitute, doing the bidding of some man who made her feel that he loved her (VII, VIII, XI, II). She *is* a prostitute in order to earn money for her

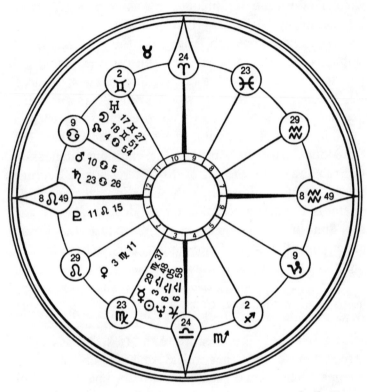

```
      C F M
      7 2 5
     F A W E
     3 7 2 2
```

boyfriend who stays at home with their baby. She wants to break out and become a pop singer.

The woman with the horoscope on page 26 has the Moon in Gemini in the XIth. Her work needs are totally wrapped up within a network of friendships and information exchange, perhaps gossip: the Moon in Gemini trines the Sun-Neptune-Jupiter conjunction in the social Sign Libra in the communications IIIrd. Mercury rules both the XIth and the IIIrd and is in its own Sign within the IIIrd. The organization of all the planets to the east suggests a strong egocentric self-awareness, emphasized by Pluto in Leo in the Ist.

Mercury is oriental: the native will just fall in line with the powerful social urges, with a routine job among her friends.

She longs desperately for emotional and home security: Saturn in Cancer in the XIIth, semi-square Venus in Virgo.

There is no opposition within the chart. The only squares are made by Mars with the Sun, Jupiter, and Neptune. Mars rules the Midheaven and is placed within the XIIth. If the woman must work (and she probably has been divorced: the Moon conjunction with Uranus, ruler of the VIIth in the love-received XIth, was activated powerfully by a Saturn-Mars conjunction transit in square at age twenty-one when the progressed Sun came to the Libra cusp of the IVth), her job would be found by following her friends. Her education had surely been interrupted (Neptune rules the IXth and is squared by Mars, as is Jupiter).

All dimensions suggest underachievement, a lack of focus and individual volition to create a specialized outlet. She is taken along by her friends, and probably works somehow in a factory (since Mars is the only planet making developmentally strong aspects and rules the Aries Midheaven).

The woman's marriage soured when she was almost twenty-one; she has a child and must work; she works with a group of friends as a machine operator in a factory. Even for her horoscope appointment, she arrived with a friend. Her major concerns are for finding another husband and home security.

In the "traditional" study of transits, the effort to be specifically all-inclusive through the ordering of planetary and aspect symbolism only confines and bewilders us. In Volume VII of this series, *Integrated Transits,* the subject was treated as a *reorganization* of developmental energies rather than an inventory of specific manifestations. This approach opens the analyst to maximum freedom in serving every individual client.

So it is with vocational analysis: there is no such thing as a planet, Sign, or aspect configuration that will determine *exactly* what work a person needs to do. Older texts often tried to categorize specific planetary professions, certain Sun-Sign proclivities. But in our more complex, modern times, when the emphasis is upon individuation, specialization, "doing your own thing," the whole must speak more than ever. As we have done throughout every volume of this series, we must follow the law of naturalness. In the study of work needs, the core identity, the Sun-Moon blend will flow throughout the whole horoscope *in terms of the work needs;* each planet will symbolically suggest a dimension, a color within the vocational portrait.

The ordering of measurements and deductions within the astrologer's mind must follow a focus of vocation; must *not* follow a singular magic measurement to establish a person's work needs. We know that the work one does is a reflection of the *whole self,* is the means through which a place in society is gained, relationships are formed, success is achieved. We must see the whole speaking through a specific level of analysis *that goes throughout the entire horoscope.*

Mercury will represent the kind of intelligence brought to the service of the job need. This measurement works closely with the diurnal speed of the Moon on the birthday to determine the mental capacity (Volume V, page 128). The initial deduction immediately keys the Sign of the Sun, the mode of life-energy expression.

Mars will represent the kind of energy that can be applied within the work situation. Saturn will describe the kind of ambition that needs to be fulfilled. Jupiter will outline the particular reward needs of the identity.

All of these come together, if the analyst will have the courage and confidence to see reflected in the horoscope *a person* in relation to an environment of experience, an identity working in life to fulfill personalized needs—rather than seeing only a maze of measurements that are supposed to conform to some

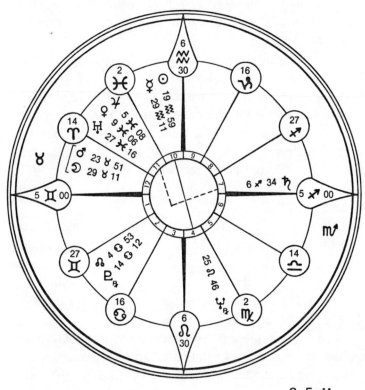

C F M
1 8 5
F A W E
2 5 4 3

☿ // ♃

absolute law of predictability. So much of life expression is based upon common sense. Analysis should be common sensical as well.

For example, in the horoscope example on page 30, from the viewpoint of character analysis, the Sun-Moon blend (Volume III) suggests that ambition is lacking, that self-contentment is too easy, that personal development is perhaps more important than grand external achievement. This man wants to develop his own private, perhaps hidden talents more than he wants to do anything externally. This deduction holds true throughout the rest of the horoscope: the Sun opposes Neptune, ruler of the XIth, within the professional axis; the emphasis is upon the eastern hemisphere; Jupiter is square Saturn, suggesting that enthusiasm is held back somehow, that it is difficult to raise goals high enough for conspicuous achievement.

Saturn powerfully placed upon the seventh cusp, gaining opposition development from the Moon, suggests that an ambitious drive would develop within the life, perhaps through a partnership with the father. The Moon develops the opposition from a conjunction in the XIIth with Mars: the ambition would grow out of an intense need to reconstruct situations along a deeply personal line, to buck established organizations and prove a personal point.

The man would be blessed with friends that would support his efforts (Venus-Jupiter conjunction square Saturn), although an emotional toll might be demanded within the man's marriage, or a break with the father at some time (an inference to be refined and tested through progressions and transits). Mercury in Aquarius would project the mind into inventive social service, echoing the Sun in the Aquarius Midheaven. The Moon, travelling at 13°23' on the day of birth, would represent average intelligence; yet, the strong Saturn in Sagittarius, ruler of the IXth and co-ruler of the Midheaven, would lift the intelligence to a high level, perhaps to an unusual level, maybe occult, reinforcing the Moon in the XIIth. That the man was born into a life of conspicuous new development is suggested strongly by the position of Mercury, ruler of the Ascendant, and the Moon in the last degree of their Signs, in precise square.

This quick character sketch *must support* fulfillment of job needs. It is the fuel for relationships with the environment through experience in work. Work is a natural extension of the whole identity.

With the Moon in the XIIth, he will want to be behind the scenes, making things happen through his own highly personal way of thinking and organizing the flow of his energy. With Saturn oriental, he will have the patience to build carefully. His personal imagination (Sun-Neptune; Saturn ruler of the IXth; XIIth House emphasis) will build the personal work structure, beginning in partnership, always influenced by others, dependent upon them (Saturn gaining opposition by the Moon).

In any horoscope, for any level of analysis, the square, opposition, or conjunction that is applying or is partile—the quadrature aspect that is closest within the horoscope—usually dominates the analysis. With judgment of vocation, this aspect is the most important as well. In this example, it is the exact Moon-Mercury square.

Mercury is in the professional Xth with the Sun and rules the Ascendant and the IInd. Its precise developmental tension with the Moon suggests that the private need of this man is to personally reconstruct his life and experience with the aim of making money. He will do this to prove something to himself. He will speculate (Mercury rules V) to make money in partnership with others within innovative public service (Mercury applies to a conjunction with Jupiter and square with Saturn). Common sense suggests that he has built a finance corporation with others, something that deals with the public financially. The man is president of several banks; his resources are over twenty million dollars.

If we were to have followed the rigid specifications of older texts, we would have been keyed by the Aquarius Midheaven and its rulers, Uranus and Saturn. We would have started thinking along the lines of scientist, inventor, astrologer, electrical specialist or real estate dealer, priest, underground worker. The specificity of reference would have denied the wholeness of this man's life needs. The key to his personal success is that he has found the right way to express his very private needs.

When did this happen within his life? At age twenty-four, while in the furniture business (Aquarius) with his father (Saturn), Mercury in progression made its station and went *retrograde,* conjunct Uranus in the XIth (goals). The client said that, at that time, a business advisor came into the family store, was retained for help, the business expanded enormously, and he learned lessons about making money that he has never forgotten. It was a crucial turning point in his life. In his own words: "I learned than that making a lot of money would be the only way I could be free." He was looking for the freedom to express the development of his inner self. Building financial security—the material destiny of this horoscope—would allow him the freedom to develop personal perspectives (Sun-Neptune opposition, Moon in the XIIth, Saturn rulership of IX, Pluto trine Venus and Jupiter from the IInd)—the spiritual destiny of the life.

At the time of horoscope analysis, progressed Mercury was stationary, turning *direct* exactly trine the natal Pluto. The fulfilled banker, at age forty-seven, is planning now to give up his holdings. He has won his freedom to seek fulfillment of other needs.

Elemental and Modal Emphasis

Deducing the choice of profession astrologically is not really complex; but the data is multi-faceted, perhaps busily textured. Starting simply, with the Moon's House position, the Sun-Moon blend, the Ascendant, the oriental planet, and then adding the Midheaven references invariably uncover a theme that describes vocational need. Transits and progressions reveal the developmental tensions accumulated within time. Common sense graces the whole with practical perspective.

Identifying Element and Mode emphasis can complement the vocational profile. In the last example, on page 30, eight points in Fixed Signs (at the expense of the Cardinal) corroborate the privacy of the man as well as his stick-to-itiveness, echoed by the Saturn oriental. With so little Cardinal emphasis, we could question leadership capacity, especially with the Moon in the XIIth. The client said, "I really don't have to be there in the banks at all; they go on without me." Pluto is the only planet in a Cardinal Sign, ruling Scorpio intercepted in the VIth: the banker planned the perspective within his job operations and that was that. And it was no surprise to learn that he has begun to study the occult to learn more about himself, how he can serve his personal needs for development that, in this case, may be strongly linked to a dimension of karma (Volume XI).

In the example on page 26, the female factory worker, the low count in Water and Earth corroborated her emotional search and her lack of practicality within it; the high count in Cardinal made her the boss of her group. All her questions were egocentric, almost paranoid, searching for some secure reference point within relationship, yet afraid to break out of the group sustaining her for the moment.

The prostitute, page 24, has only Venus in a Mutable Sign: with this Venus exactly trine Uranus, embracing the whole planetary configuration of the horoscope, Venus ruling the Midheaven, she is extremely vulnerable through an appeal to her emotions. The promise of love from her boyfriend was strong enough, within her only supportive aspect, to push her into prostitution, *his* choice (her Moon in VIII). With only the Ascendant in an Earth Sign, it was extremely difficult to bring a practical anchor to the total southern hemisphere configuration.

The ballerina, page 22, has a blend of Cardinal and Mutable, suggesting the inspired and yet flexible artist with no set constructs that would inhibit her spontaneity of creation or her absorption of choreographers' suggestions. With only Mars in an Earth Sign in the XIIth, she was indeed impractical, often overworking herself to exhaustion in developing technique and once to the point of a serious foot injury.

Saturn and Jupiter

Ambition is fulfilled, the person recognizes success through reward. The symbolisms of Saturn and Jupiter are definitely closely allied. Even their transit periods are significant together, since Jupiter (twelve years) will be opposing its birth position (awareness of opportunity) when Saturn (thirty) makes its first return; Jupiter will have returned to its birth position for the third time at thirty-six when Saturn makes the opening square to its birth position in its second orbit (see Volume VII, page 32). Ambition and opportunity must be in harmony within work fulfillment.

For example, the banker (page 30) has Saturn in Sagittarius. The needs of the ambition are to exploit a higher mind level, to master a philosophy of life. He has Jupiter in Pisces. What he needs to feel successful, to feel rewarded through expressing ambition, must suit a private, unassuming, personal feeling or dream. There is a very fine balance here, and we have seen that this goal of the ambition and hope for personal reward were the major private theme of his life, that the freedom to fulfill this theme was the objective of the work needs related to the precise square between Mercury and the Moon (the Moon was applying to square with Jupiter and opposition to Saturn within life development).

For Patricia Hearst (page 18), the ambition would reflect˙ the deepest workings of self-organization, accompanied by complex defenses (Saturn in Scorpio). Giving of herself would be extremely difficult because of the tight structure. Externalization would be difficult. The rewards required by this difficult ambition profile would be in terms of Jupiter in Gemini: diversity and travel would replace conventionality; new opinions would be gathered by this receptive Piscean (with Mutable Angles). Ambition would be fulfilled through inquiry and adventure. With enough avenues travelled, she would find focus and outlet for her ambition. Patricia Hearst could never have endured within a set mold of behavior. The complex and frustrated needs of her ambition were too great.

The prostitute (page 24) also has Saturn in Scorpio, the same ambition-need profile as Patricia Hearst, but her reward-need profile is different. Jupiter in Leo suggests that personal appreciation is needed even more than financial remuneration. She cares nothing about the income gained through the work she has chosen, through the potential income from the career she desires as a pop singer. She wants only to be loved, to be adored by her mate, to be thought of as personally valuable through her musical potential. This great need for personal appreciation has been expanded out of perspective (Jupiter

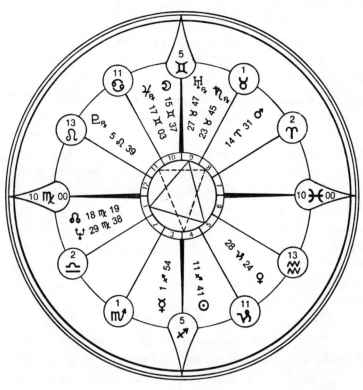

CFM
2 3 9
FAWE
5 4 0 5

conjunct Pluto and the Moon in VIII; Jupiter is dispositor of Venus) and is the limitation upon her self-development (Jupiter rules Sagittarius on the XIIth).

Governor Nelson Rockefeller has Saturn in Aries and Jupiter in Leo: his ambition is to be number one, but this drive, this need, carries with it a curious open apology for its exposed nature, its manifested strength (Volume III). His hope for reward is in terms of personal appreciation, personal recognition. The symbologies mesh perfectly. His horoscope has a Libra Ascendant. His Sun is in Cancer conjunct Neptune (just like President Ford's). His Moon is in Scorpio and in the Ist House (as Truman's was). All these observations corroborate one another. He has nine points Cardinal, four Fixed, and only Pluto Mutable.

The example on page 38 is the horoscope of a young man employed by the city government as a personnel interviewer. He presents himself amiably yet introvertedly (retrogradation emphasis, Earth Grand Trine; Volume V). There is a pronounced emphasis upon the Mutable Signs and an absence of Water accent. He is trying to find his place in the world, a goal with which he can identify and gain emotional significance. The Fire Grand Trine reflects his sustaining, secure circuit of work energy. The Earth Grand Trine (without the Sun or Moon) suggests his practical self-sufficiency. His ambition is to find a structure for himself, but he does not know what kind. His hope for reward (Jupiter in Gemini) is for diversity and adventure within his work, "to improve myself," he says with great objectivity about himself.

Mercury rules the Gemini Midheaven and the Virgo

Ascendant. Mercury is oriental and is related to both Grand Trine circuits through the sextile with Neptune and the opposition to Uranus, through the trine with Pluto and the applying conjunction with the Sun. Mercury is also in mutual reception with Jupiter, dispositor of the Sun. There is no doubt that Mercury is the most important planet in this horoscope.

Mercury in Sagittarius suggests an accelerated thought process, a nervous opinionatedness (especially with the Gemini emphasis and Virgo upon the Ascendant). The introversion factors and the containment of the two Grand Trines modify this nervousness considerably. In the stabilization process, judgment is improved.

Mercury is in its natural House, the IIIrd. The Mutable Sign Sagittarius and the Cadent House suggest great reaction potential within the personality. Scorpio on the cusp of the IIIrd keys Pluto, its ruler, within the Fire Grand Trine. The Sun within the same construct is the dispositor of Pluto. The analysis, through concentration upon Mercury and the IIIrd House, begins to reveal writing dimensions.

I simply said to the client, "You know, Peter, you are a writer." Immediately this triggered a different personality. Peter became expressive, articulate, voluble. He loved to write! Writing papers in college had been his major accomplishment. (Subsequently, he sent me copies of much of what he had written, and his work was excellent.)

But what kind of writing would he do best? With the Moon in the Xth, he was a take-charge person of highly keen reactability (Sun-Moon polarity). The two Grand Trines made him very self-sufficient. He had great critical abilities through Mercury and its rulerships, through its oriental position as well. Pluto's position within the Grand Trine and as ruler of the IIIrd cusp keyed thoughts of research.

I suggested that his real skill was as a research writer in marketing analysis or in undercover work. He replied that he had already applied to the Central Intelligence Agency for such a job! This was the work profile that would satisfy Peter's self-sufficient strengths, his writing skill, his critical judgment strengths, and his needs for diversity and independence. Transits and progressions then determined the best time for him to make the change of profession (suggested by the duality Midheaven as well) and start again in the right direction toward success.

His present job as personnel interviewer hardly broke the surface of his potential, although this job too was keyed to information exchange, research, communication, independence, and diversity.

Relocation

As we have seen in the study of Solar Revolutions (Volume VII), an exciting premise yet to be conclusively verified is suggested by applying astrology systematically to the conduct of life: that man can adjust his year to come, his life to come, by changing locations upon his birthday, by relocating for a long period of time in a place yielding improved astrological configurations. The premise is quite specific with regard to the study of success within

Natal

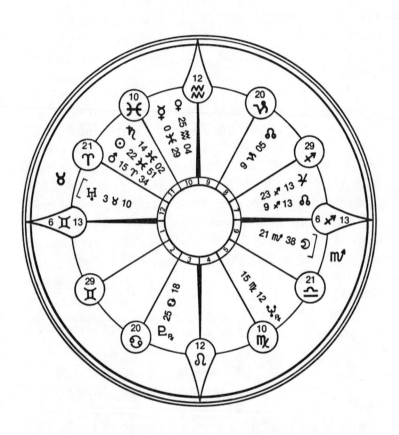

work: relocation will adjust the House cusps and place the birth configuration into different experiential perspective. In our modern day, when relocation is practically the rule rather than the exception, perhaps this premise is a very important consideration. Finding new direction and location is certainly a very common objective within astrologer-client relationships.

To recompute the House cusps for a new location is a very easy operation: simply adjust the actual birth time from the place of birth to the place of planned relocation; recompute the House cusps through Sidereal-Time correction *as if the native were born at the same moment but in the different location.* The adjustment is simply a change of time-zones, longitude and latitude.

The example shown on page 42 is the horoscope of an executive born at 9:30 A.M. EST. He relocated to Düsseldorf, Germany, six hours eastward, six hours *later* in clock time. When the man was born at 9:30 A.M. EST, it was 3:30 P.M. in Germany, Middle European Standard Time. On page 44 the relocation chart is shown. Note: the planetary positions remain the same, only the demarcation of the cusps changes.

In the relocation chart, the Ascendant becomes very strong in Leo, trined by Jupiter in Sagittarius in the relocation Vth (speculation). The Moon gains angularity in the IVth. The executive worked for a large international American firm (Moon in IV, homeland, trine the Sun in VIII, others' resources).

Venus in the relocation chart becomes ruler of its Midheaven and is placed in the VIIth. The executive is a

Relocation to Düsseldorf 51 N — 7 E
Born: 9:30 AM, EST; 3:30 PM, MET

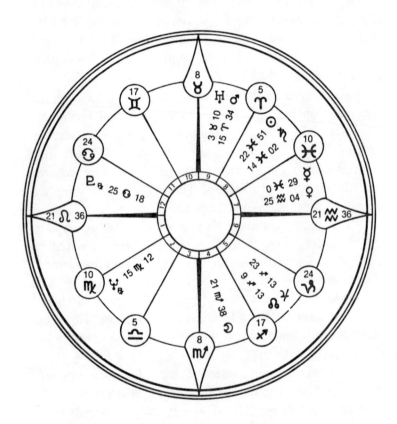

Natal

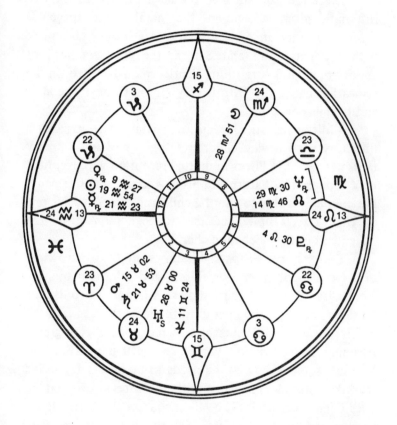

sales director, and Venus rules the IIIrd House of the relocation chart as well (as the Moon does in the natal).

The relocation fulfilled the need for reward through internationalism shown in the natal chart (page 42) through Jupiter in Sagittarius, in developmental square with the natal Sun and Saturn; the direction need of ambition, natal Saturn ruling Capricorn on the IXth. In the relocation chart, the IXth is very strong through the Mars and Uranus positions.

Additionally, the executive's natal chart suggests a difficulty with having children (Virgo on V and Mercury in its detriment in Pisces in mutual reception with Neptune in V, opposed by Saturn). In his new location in Germany, the couple was able to adopt a child and then conceive one of their own (Jupiter in its own Sign in V, trine the Ascendant of the relocation chart).

The example on page 45 shows the birth horoscope of a German born in Düsseldorf who relocated to New York City. The natal chart shows an important conflict, a tension that drives the man to fulfillment: the Sun is in the XIIth House with Venus and Mercury, both retrograde. Although he is "held in," nervously "bottled up" (Sun and Mercury square Uranus), he needs to be on display in his work, identified personally with the success of what he does (Venus oriental). The Moon squares the XIIth House group and opposes Mars, Saturn, and Uranus. The discharge of this T Cross is into the late part of the VIth House. He works extremely hard, is kept behind the scenes of his company, projects a philosophy of his own upon company potentials, is always on the verge of creating animosity with his superiors because of his great desire to break out into the open. He feels himself indispensable to the company, but has difficulty gaining fulfillment, recognition, success.

A major relocation took place with Saturn's transit return to its natal position. The young man looked for a new job, was successful, and was transferred to New York City, fulfilling the promise of the Moon in IX, Scorpio's ruler in VI in wide opposition to the Sun and sextile to Jupiter, ruler of the Midheaven.

The relocation chart for New York (page 48) shows improvement of the work situation for the man: the Sun, Mercury and Venus are taken out of the XIIth, Mercury becoming ruler of the relocation Xth. Neptune is brought into the Xth and is very positive through the trine to Saturn and Uranus and sextile with the Moon. Jupiter becomes ruler of the relocation Ascendant and is placed in the VIIth of the relocation chart, still trine Venus and the Sun, of course.

The only difficulty is that the Moon is placed in the XIIth, again locating the man behind the scenes. The man became assistant to the president of an international firm, but simply wasn't given responsibility commensurate with the job title. When he communicated his views, he seemed to upset the organization. It appeared that his main value was his bilingual ability, and the relocation chart appeared to suggest this with the strong IIIrd House.

The executive again changed jobs, joining another international firm, and relocated to Asheville, North Carolina. There wasn't much change in the relocation chart

Relocation to New York City, 74 W – 41 N
Birth: 8:10 AM, MET; 2:10 AM, EST

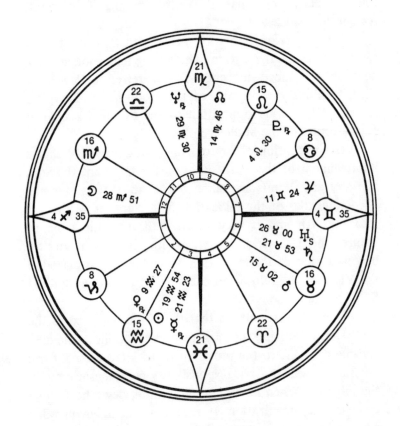

Relocation to Asheville, N.C., 82 W 30 -- 35 N 40
Birth: 8:10 AM, MET; 2:10 AM, EST

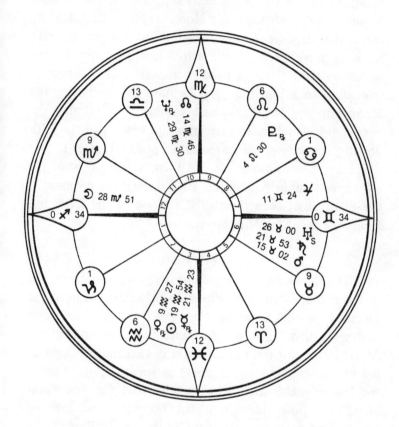

(page 49). He will travel a great deal as he did in his first job (IIIrd House emphasis, the Sun ruling the IXth; Sagittarius upon the Ascendant; Jupiter in the VIIth, trine Venus and the Sun), but his Moon is still in the XIIth. We can anticipate that the same frustrations will remain. With his next move, perhaps with astrological guidance, he can make a giant step toward personal success through relocation to a longitude and latitude that will bring the Moon into the Ist. Thereafter, we could project that the next move would be to place the Sun angular in the IVth or Xth, suggesting a high executive position, after he has gained the experience and success of strategic self-expression in foreign lands, fulfilling the promise in the birth chart seen through the Moon in the IXth and Jupiter's rule of the Midheaven.

Review

The following ten partial horoscopes will give practice to the eye in establishing direction of vocational need for success in work fulfillment. When pertinent, the horoscope outlines will be filled out for more complete delineation. At all times, we must *accumulate* deductions throughout the key measurements pertaining to vocation, based upon the law of naturalness, the premise that the Sun-Moon blend will flow throughout the horoscope network of aspects and rulerships *consistently*. When the level of our inspection is vocational choice with the goal of success through need fulfillment, the entire horoscope must adhere to this line of inspection.

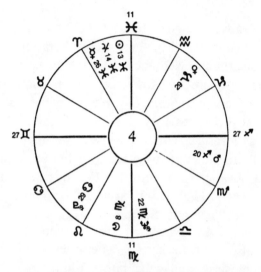

Example 4: This woman has the Sun in Pisces and the Moon in Virgo: "discriminating intellect communicates the sensitive intuition. An imbalance within this opposition from aspects elsewhere in the horoscope can break the bond between intellect and intuition. Then, one feels lonely in every crowd" (Volume III). We look into the horoscope, following this Sun-Moon blend, its natural flow throughout the identity in terms of vocational choice: the Pisces Midheaven alerts us to a possible dual profession, reinforced by the Sun's opposition with Neptune, angular, and the Gemini Ascendant. The Sun's position with Jupiter and Mercury within the opposition with Neptune reinforces the deduction of imaginative intellect. The Moon position in III suggests the vocational need to be a go-between, a communicator, with great precision and

perhaps idealism (Virgo). Mercury and Neptune in mutual reception takes us still further to corroboration (Mercury rules the Ascendant; Neptune rules the Midheaven).

Mars is square the X-IV axis: a tremendous reactant reservoir of energy within the work experiences. Venus, ruler of the Vth (creativity, teaching), is sextile Mercury, always a measurement of artistic sensitivity. Venus opposes Pluto exactly, suggesting a grand expenditure of emotional awareness, of intuition (Venus rules Taurus on XII), within the work style, the immediate job environment (Pluto rules Scorpio on VI).

We begin to sense that this woman is an artist, perhaps also a teacher; a go-between of emotional, aesthetic, musical, intellectual information.

She is an international opera singer and *was* a professor of mathematics! Her approach to singing is through a mathematical exactness (Moon in Virgo). A strange relationship with her mother, by whom she feels constantly pushed, has inhibited her emotional growth and given her a loneliness within her fame. The deductions are completed by her Saturn in Aries in XI; she is every bit the prima donna (Aries), yet always apologetic about her success, often appearing hypochondriacal, in grand need for love and attention (Saturn in XI).

Example 5: This male has the Sun in Gemini and the Moon in Aquarius: "the unusual and innovating dimensions of Aquarius give to the mentality a keen insight and foresight. Intuition for things, people, and situations gives facile expression to the intellect. These are

the Sun and Moon positions of the humanitarian"
(Volume III).

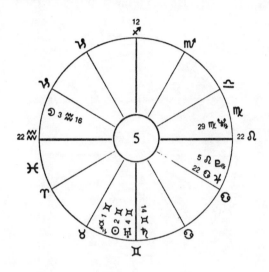

With Mercury in its own Sign and in conjunction with
the Sun and Uranus, ruler of the Ascendant, in the IIIrd,
Gemini's natural House, there is no doubt that this man's
projection of self will be through communication. With the
prominence of Uranus, we immediately must consider
broadcasting (electricity) and some kind of prediction,
innovation, unusualness. This is corroborated by the
Sun-Moon blend and the trine between the IIIrd House
group and Neptune in the VIIth; by the Moon's opposition
with Pluto in the VIth, ruler of the IXth, Jupiter's natural
House, with Jupiter also in the VIth. The man is a natural
communicator. His Moon in the XIIth shows that he wants
to be behind the scenes, yet the opposition with Pluto

draws out this perspective and the trine III-VII gives outlet for it all through the public in a theatrical way (Leo on VII; Neptune in VII). He is a television weatherman.

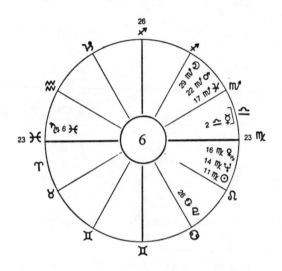

Example 6: With the Sun in Virgo and the Moon in Scorpio, this man can easily lose realism in self-appraisal. The emotions can overexaggerate self-importance. This deduction is born out through the close conjunction of the Sun and Neptune, which rules the Pisces Ascendant. This conjunction will dominate the man vocationally since the Sun rules Leo on the VIth and Neptune rules the Ascendant. Venus as well is involved with the conjunction and rules Libra intercepted in the VIIth and Taurus on the IInd (self-worth, income). Initially, one would have to regard this man as an artist of some kind.

The Moon is in VIII: the vocational need would be to

reorganize the work of others, to depend on what is done by others for personal expression. There is strong indication that there would be a strong duality within the profession: the opposition of the VIth House group to Saturn in *Pisces,* retrograde in XII. Additionally, Venus is retrograde in VI.

The man stated that he was a land broker, at a very high level economically. I replied that he was certainly also an artist. Indeed, he had for a long time been an artist, had become dissatisfied with his own artistic ability, and had developed into an artist's representative (Moon in VIII). This salesmanship ability was corroborated by Mercury, ruler of III, in VII in Libra, but making no significant aspect with any body within the horoscope.

The shift in profession had preserved· the salesmanship and reorganization functions but had shifted emphasis within the dominant opposition from the Sun-Neptune pole to the Saturn. Then, reading the symbols at the land broker level, Mercury gained prominence as ruler of IV (land), placed in VII, public presentation; Saturn became real estate; Uranus, added in II, in Taurus, trine the VIth House group, completed the picture. Pluto oriental corroborated his desire to meet the big dealers in the land market, to gain personal prestige and power through helping them reorganize land acquisition, etc. (Pluto trine the VIIIth House group and in mutual reception with the Moon).

Example 7: This young woman has a strong III-IX axis with Mercury opposed Saturn, suggesting terrific mental awareness and precocious mental seriousness. Venus, dispositor of Saturn, ruler of the international IXth and dispositor of the Sun and the Moon, immediately brings internationalism into mind for the projection of the whole self. This is corroborated further by Jupiter's rulership of the Ascendant (again, internationalism, learning) and Jupiter's conjunction with the Sun. Jupiter oriental would suggest lots of enthusiasm here, rushing perhaps to get the job done quickly, cramming much study into her college curriculum. The Moon is just leaving the IVth entering the Vth: her great need is to accept things as they are and become intensely aware of them, in communication channels. The young woman is studying to be an interpreter in three languages all at the same time. She has inherited this intense desire from her mother who works within the home as a language instructor.

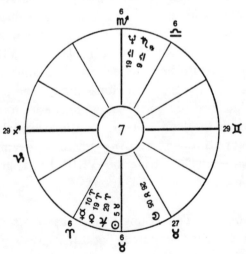

The Sun-Moon blend described in Volume III suggests that she will respect her studies and rigorous disciplines in order *to become an authority herself.*

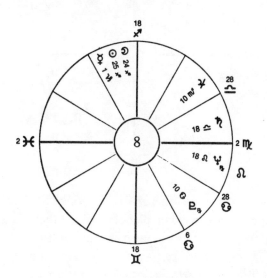

Example 8: Strong intellectual, philosophical energy is suggested by the New Moon in Sagittarius. The Moon is oriental, suggesting a sense of collective concern. He will take charge of the professional situation (Moon in X), projecting his ideas upon the public to guide or help them. He is enormously perceptive (Mercury in Capricorn within orb of the Sun-Moon conjunction is sextile the Ascendant). Saturn in Libra gives us an additional social dimension in the projection of ambition, especially within the VIIth House and sextile the Sun and Moon. This Saturn is also sextile Neptune, which is trine the Sun and Moon. Neptune is in the VIth, the House of services.

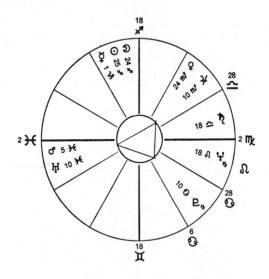

The man is a doctor. Let's look further at the horoscope with the other planets added: there is a Grand Trine in Water not involving the Sun or the Moon. The doctor is extremely self-sufficient, emotionally in his personal life and perhaps somehow within his vocational practice. The closest aspects within the chart are among Uranus, Jupiter, and Pluto within the Grand Trine. There would be a highly individualistically developed emotional construct that would dominate this man's whole life. It would issue into his profession through the applying square between Jupiter within the Grand Trine and Neptune trine the Xth House group. This shows through all his isolation professionally within research, his devotion to work in service of others.

The VIth becomes extremely important as the liaison between the only square in the horoscope and the dominating trines. The VIth is the natural House of Virgo, here placed upon the VIIth. Mercury in Capricorn in conjunction with the Sun and Moon in X would link the VIth House significances within the analysis to the doctor's diagnostic ability. The concerns of diet, nutrition, the intestines, natural foods (Virgo; the VIth) would have to be evaluated. The final deduction confirms this: the Moon rules Cancer on the VIth and the Sun disposes of Neptune in the VIth. The doctor is an emotional hermit, divorced; has social and sexual relationships almost exclusively with women he meets in his practice; he is a renowned specialist in homeopathy, natural healing through herbs, salts, minerals.

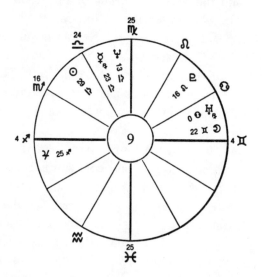

Example 9: This man's Sun in Libra and Moon in Gemini suggest a voluble, social personality, expressive and

articulate. There is ease in socializing, and his audience is never displeased. He is a "romantic." The challenge is to link ease of expression with a substantive mission—corroborated by the Moon in VII.

With the Moon applying to conjunction with Uranus, ruler of III, we begin to anticipate some unusualness in social, public communication. Jupiter, ruler of the Ascendant, is in opposition with the Moon, suggesting a philosophical awareness dominating the personality projection. The Moon's trine with Neptune, Mercury, and the Sun introduces Neptune's rulership of IV, the Moon's rulership of VIII, and Mercury's rulership of the Midheaven and the VIIth, disposing of the Moon. Pluto in VIII is ruler of XII and sextiles Neptune, Mercury, and the Sun, and trines Jupiter. The matrix of the unconscious (Volume V) is in sharp accentuation here (Houses IV, VIII, XII; the trans-Saturnian planets; the Moon). This man must be in tune with the higher mind (Sun rules IX; Mercury's retrogradation). He is a professional psychic.

Example 10: With the Sun in Aries and the Moon in Capricorn, "heated ambition and cold administration have a developmental tension that almost inevitably creates success. Forceful expression is anchored" (Volume III). Mars is oriental, further suggesting "the promoter." The Sun is applying to a conjunction with Uranus, ruler of the Midheaven, suggesting the strong individualistic development within career expression. Strangely, with such ego emphasis, the Moon is in the IXth, indicating that the individuality itself is *de*-emphasized, that a spectrum of higher values enters into study. This is reinforced through Saturn's placement in the IXth, in Aquarius, giving a humanitarian profile to the needs of personal ambition.

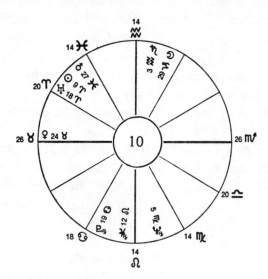

The Moon is trine Venus in Taurus upon the Ascendant. The man has to be an artist, a painter, whose ego speaks through his works.

What kind of painter is he? The Sun and Uranus both trine Jupiter in III (communications); the Sun and Uranus both square Pluto in III (the House ruled by the Moon), ruler of VII. He paints extremely large canvases, with a grand scope of public projection and social perspective.

Interestingly, Neptune seems uninvolved within this artist's horoscope profile—at first glance. But Neptune is the only planet angular and it is in a dynamic aspect configuration called "the finger of Yod" or the "finger of

God." This configuration occcurs when one planet (here, Neptune) makes a quincunx aspect (150°, five Signs) with two other planets (here, Sun and Saturn) which are in sextile. This configuration comes close to an indication of destiny, to a fatalistic fulfillment within the experiences suggested by the configuration. Here, the discharge point is within the Xth, opposite Neptune (always opposite the "finger"; at the midpoint between the planets in sextile).[1]

The man is definitely destined to be an artist.

Example 11: With the Sun in Taurus and the Moon in Libra, there will be a tension within the personality between a solid, things-are-as-they-are posture and a social projection that is needed for individual self-gratification. This is reinforced by the Moon's position within the XIth.

The Sun rules the Xth and is placed in the VIIth, along with Mars oriental, Pluto (ruler of the Ascendant), and Venus in its own Sign and disposing of the Moon. Saturn in Capricorn in the communications IIIrd trines the entire VIIth House group: this is a wise man, whose communication to the public is recognized as socially and humanistically aware. The structure of things-as-they-are blends

---

1. The "finger of Yod" configuration will be discussed in full in Volume XI of this series.

superbly with the awareness of the social cause (the Moon trines the VIIth House group from across the Sign line in Libra). The man could well be a social writer, a social commentator. With Jupiter and Uranus in conjunction within the Moon's Sign in the IXth, sextile the VIIth House group, the dimension of unusual philosophy is also suggested.

The concepts of time (Saturn), communication, research (Scorpio), an authoritative position (Leo), and enormous social awareness all blend to make this the horoscope of a social historian. It is part of the horoscope of Bertrand Russell, who, even in his 90's, was picketing for social causes.

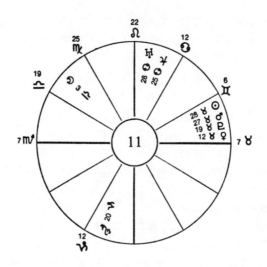

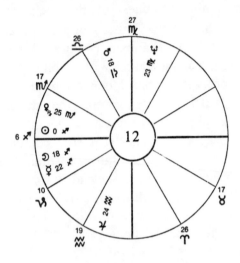

Example 12: This young woman needs "to do her own thing" (Moon in I). The Moon applies to a conjunction with Mercury (ruler of X) and square with Neptune. Her daydreams, her fantasies will be the source of her job orientation. Venus is dispositor of Mars in X and is retrograde in Scorpio in XII: a very private sense of beauty (Volume II) and deep awareness of religious or occult "beauties" may inhibit her success in expression (XIIth House Venus and Sun; Venus square Jupiter in III, ruler of the Ascendant). Yet the developmental tension seen in the Venus square with Jupiter will eventually be the support of her individual talent since Venus sextiles Neptune and Jupiter is in trine with Mars. It is not surprising that this woman espoused an avant-garde religion, wrote stories and songs for her faith, finally left

the faith, ended her marriage, and now is concentrating upon writing children's stories and music (Mars rules V).

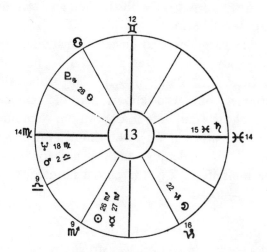

Example 13: The Sun-Moon blend suggests strength, magnetism, and "savvy," perhaps a hard-driving application of self-aware strategies: "the man who is important is the man to please." The plight of the underdog may give a challenge to the personal discovery-and-fight mechanisms. Opinions become strategies to be weighed.

The Sun in the IIIrd (Mercury's natural House) with Mercury, which also rules the Ascendant and the Midheaven, immediately suggests a communicator, through whom would flow the energies suggested by the Sun-Moon blend. The Moon in the Vth would definitely show a sensationalizing of everyday experiences, a theatrical bent. With the Moon opposing Pluto, dispositor of the Sun and Mercury, the perspective of the theatrical is extremely attentuated. Pluto is trine with the Sun and Mercury; the Moon disposes of Pluto.

Neptune rising gives an imagination and sensitivity to the theatricality; Virgo gives a precision, the bon mot, perhaps. There is no doubt that this horoscope belongs to an entertainer, one who knows that the public is the "man" to please (Pluto-Moon opposition; Neptune ruling Pisces on VII; Saturn in VII), who through life experiences champions the underdog and is perhaps often the underdog himself. This is the partial horoscope of Dick Cavett.

Conclusion

Older texts in Astrology strove to be rock-solid specific in delineation. Even today, many research efforts are directed at finding the "magic measurements" that will infallibly delineate deductions of life potential and experience. All these efforts are to be lauded, but, at the same time, the effort to establish the *science* of Astrology must not overwhelm the challenge to be *artistic*. The miracle of individuality is rendered comprehensible more through art than through science. The magic measurements that synthesize a horoscope *are within us,* the astrologers, within our sharing of meanings with our clients. When the coefficient pi is finally adjusted to a whole number, perhaps then can we expect an absolutism of measurement within Astrology. Until then, the indeterminateness of nature must be respected and appreciated in terms of relativity, interrelationship. The function of pi is to adjust the relationships within the circle, and this measurement of relativity is enough for the scientist to place a man upon the Moon.

For example, if we were to seek out the astrological configurations associated with a person high in the banking profession, we would immediately think of Taurus, its ruler Venus, the IInd House—the indices that specifically have to do with money. We might acknowledge that the Vth House would be important if the speculative portion of banking and investments were involved. Immediately, we can begin to see all the Signs' significances within the full spectrum of banking: the Aries, Cancer, Libra and Capricorn emphases within the banking profession would have a specific kind of energy modality; the organizational attributes would be different within banking for Taurus, Leo, Scorpio, and Aquarius; the reaction potentials would be different for Gemini, Virgo, Sagittarius, Pisces. All these Signs are important in their own ways. Perhaps statistically, there are more Taureans within banking than any other Sign, but that really tells us very little. It is the whole matrix of needs within the individual horoscope that will be fulfilled by the banking profession. An individual is *all Signs.* It is the analyst's common-sense deductions from many variables that hopefully will capture the individual's whole inclination.

Only when a specific Sign, specific House, and/or specific planet is highly prominent can we expect corroboration of significator generalities. The two

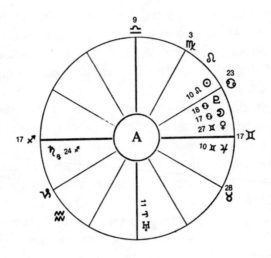

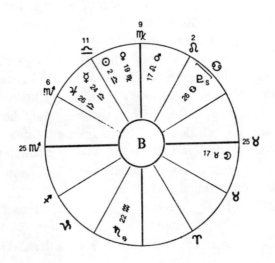

horoscope outlines on page 68 are of two men at the top of the banking profession. Each is globally prominent in his institutional position.

Banker A has the Sun in Leo and the Moon in Cancer, suggesting strong self-assurance, and easy projection of the self. The Sun in close trine with angular Uranus strengthens the initial deductions greatly, certainly promising success, perhaps a presidential position.

The Moon in VII suggests the public personality and, on the personal level, someone to whom marriage, home security, family love will be very important, perhaps as a base for his exalted public achievement potential.

With Pluto oriental, we know that the Leo drive to prominence will be extremely powerful, that knowing the "right" people, gaining personal power will be important within the job and to the job development. Jupiter rules the Ascendant and sextiles the Sun and Uranus from the VIth.

Venus rules the Midheaven and is in awareness opposition with Saturn, the only body in the eastern hemisphere. Saturn rules Capricorn and, with Uranus, Aquarius; both these Signs mark the IInd House. Venus, the natural ruler of the second and here ruler of the Midheaven, also rules Taurus on the VIth. This case *is* classic: the man must be a banker.

With this deduction firm, we can add nuance: the VIIIth becomes other peoples' resources; Cancer alerts us to savings, the holdings of money for security; the prominence of Saturn in Sagittarius, the potentials of Leo all suggest government, politics. This powerful man is involved with all these activities intensely.

Banker B has the Sun in Libra and the Moon in Taurus, suggesting that personality and social dimensions will be the identity's strongest assets. Venus oriental corroborates this, indicating that he will be a society "showman," earning his success through his personal presentation.

Jupiter rules Sagittarius on II and is placed in XI in Libra, again corroborating the social-friendship base for job success. Venus becomes all-important as the dispositor of the Sun, Jupiter, the Moon, and ruling the VIth. Venus is in mutual reception with Mercury, ruler of the Midheaven. Banking is suggested.

The Sun rules Leo on the IXth, and Mars in Leo in IX semi-squares the Sun exactly and squares the Moon exactly. Pluto rules the Ascendant and squares Jupiter exactly. These measurements definitely suggest that the profession of banking would involve foreign markets, that the energy could be best applied abroad, further corroborated by the Mars opposition with Saturn in Aquarius, Saturn ruling Capricorn intercepted within the IInd House.

International banker B is a different kind of banker than savings banker A; he's a different kind of man. Both have different homelives, different ways of emotional expression, different needs that are fulfilled in different ways through basically the same profession.

It would be impossible for either of these two men to be anything but top men in their field. The full horoscopes reveal no debilitating problems, no sociological depression, no interruption of education. Each does have personal tensions and life traumas (not shown in the horoscope sketches) that *mobilized* their ascent and achievement. For banker A, the motivation is for personal power to fulfill a keen, almost ministerial (Saturn) social-political ethic; for banker B, the motivation is to work with his personal magnetism to eventually uncover the meaning of his charisma, of emotional expression, to understand things as they are (Scorpio Ascendant). Banker B has no external mission as banker A does; rather, he really is working to understand himself.

The job of delineating vocation is easier the more developed the individual has become, the more thoroughly in use the whole horoscope is. It is easier to spot a battalion on the move than a platoon.

The major difficulty for the astrologer in his or her service is in delineating a profession or a work direction for an individual who has not had full educational opportunity or who has a particularly debilitating problem in the life. The most difficult case is the person (usually a woman) who has been idle many years within the house, who (through transits and progressions) becomes eager to do something outside the home and has no particularly refined skill to serve the motivation. These are usually "low tension" horoscopes (horoscopes with no opposition or only one square or heavy introversion measurements) or horoscopes where the tensions have been covered over, unacknowledged, sublimated.

In these cases, it is folly to project a line of work that satisfies inclination but cannot be supported by developed strengths. Here, volunteer services within the community become important: such work, such diversion often will help raise self-esteem, get the individual circulating, help the person feel better about himself or herself. Adult education courses often serve the need for self-esteem very well. Hobbies developed along the lines indicated through the horoscope and during dialogue with the client often work beautifully to give the individual a more crystallized identity.

Work, self-application, sharing of self are one and the same. They are deep personal needs fulfilled through relationships outside the self. What a person does for a living reflects the person's worth, achievement, significance, purpose. The standard against which self-esteem is measured is within the horoscope, i.e., the potentials for self-projection revealed through it. When men and women work to fulfill these potentials, they are working toward success. And as every philosophy acknowledges, to fulfill potentials is the definition of greatness.

But every philosophy must somehow acknowledge reality. The realities of today present us with many very difficult problems: many people are unemployed, and the employment rate reflects the health and stability of the nation; students in universities face a spectrum of courses that often bewilders rather than focuses student development; gaining admission to universities is becoming more and more difficult; educational standards are being lowered in a wave of excessive diversity, supposed modern educational concepts; sociological tensions are still with us.

In the early phase of the Aquarian Age, the emphasis upon individuality is overdone, is perhaps over-focused within an unstable, diffused reality: "doing your own thing" works to break up stratified work patterns. The era's demand for individuality simply does not bring out the best in many individuals, does not gain an echo from many horoscopes.

Many young people, especially those with Uranus square Pluto, those a little older with Uranus square Neptune, those in between with Saturn conjunct Pluto and those older still with Saturn opposed Neptune—these young people whose *generational aspects are linked to the inner-will planets* are facing highly individual challenges to do their thing *in a specialized, highly individualized way.* Each generation has its dimensions of individualized unrest. For many, the resources of society, its expectations, its opportunities, its disciplines *do not fit the individual's self-concept.* Is there room within vocational reality for all these indivicual needs?

The hardest challenge to the astrologer is to meet someone who professes to know exactly what he or she wants to do, needs to do—knows it emphatically—yet the goal simply does not fit the individual potentials shown in the horoscope and framed within reality. Perhaps education has been abandoned, society confines or gives too much freedom, circumstances of individual need do not match the circumstances of reality. Every astrologer meets time and time again the drop-out, the rebel, the person whose financial inheritance insulates societal relationships and veils personal fulfillment. In these cases, the Moon position, the oriental planet, and the synthesis are lost in another frame of reference.

The problem is one of level. At what level is the individual functioning? On the one hand, we know that the will must make mistakes before disciplines are internalized, before the will itself is strengthened. This is why horoscopes studied before Saturn's first return to its birth position are more difficult to understand than those studied after the age of 28 or 30.

The problem of level must establish a perspective for astrologers. The first dimension of this perspective is how much the client has done with his or her life so far; the second dimension is how expressive of the individual horoscope has that progress been; the third dimension is how do goals match possibilities within resources, individual responsibilities, and sociological reality. The astrologer's perspective then must *adjust* analysis to the concept of level: not everyone can be doctor, banker, artist, revolutionary, or astrologer. Perhaps the hobby or intrafamilial role will become the major expression of individuality potential: caring for the family as a doctor or nurse, or volunteering for hospital service within the community, or even marrying someone in the medical profession; managing family finances, investing in the stock market, holding forth energetically at parties in criticism of national finances; redecorating the home, painting pictures, spending six months designing the family's Christmas card; leading local labor groups, working for political campaigns in spare time; spending all private time in the study of Astrology and the occult. The level of the individual life in its free time, the time it calls its own, may be the more significant area of the life—beyond, separate from the external relationship established through the job within society. Perhaps it is only there that the individual can really *be*.

Magazines often report the taxi-cab driver who is an expert on Egyptology or some other esoteric subject, the stevedore who has mastered the classics of philosophy, the recluse who invents incredible machines or sweeps the stock market, the housewife whose energy in the community puts a political candidate into office, the local groups who bring pressure upon the government to effect social change. These people—simply even through listening to music or reading books—*establish themselves*, separate from the job situation in reality. Their individual levels, because of an interruption in education, heavy family responsibilities, parental influence, a health crisis, societal confinements, are fulfilled in their own *free* time, when relationship essentials through the job are met at one level and the true potentials are fulfilled at a level much different, away from societal expectations. Revealingly, these individuals refer to their private times, their highly individualized areas of life, as their "claim to fame." And we must note that work days, work weeks are becoming shorter: leisure time is becoming a strong social challenge, opportunity, and responsibility.

A final, jarringly realistic dimension of the astrologer's perspective must be that there *are* "losers" in the world: people who are or feel that they are born at the wrong time. Perhaps in these cases, the answer lies in an understanding of karma (Volume XI), a philosophy that also recognizes potentials, need, relationship, discipline, and fulfillment.

2

Sex

As the depth of primal energy and the apex of procreative responsibility, sex is the great mystery. Through sex, the human organism fulfills biological function and establishes personal identity by creation of a facsimile. To be of service in counselling, therefore, the astrologer must be sensitive to the sexual dimension of the horoscope and must be able to deal frankly with it. But vestiges of a repressive past and pressures of an emancipated present complicate astrological service. The astrologer must be aware of the tensions generated by conflicts between past and present. A tension surrounds sex, chiefly in three areas.

First: social evolution to the present has somehow created a separation between sex and love. The degree of separation is not definite or constant. It varies with era, religion, culture, individuals, and hierarchial need constructs within developing experience.

We speak easily of the debauchery of ancient societies; the Victorianism of the last century; the

Freudian era; the Romantics; the freedoms of the 1960's and 70's. All eras embrace the individuals living within them and, astrologically, are understandable through the interrelationships of the planets Jupiter, Saturn, Uranus, Neptune, and Pluto. Astrologers of historical sophistication can see many parallels between "Grand Conjunctions," between "Grand Mutations" and changes within historical eras (Volume XI). Individual horoscopes that "internalize" these era-measurements through aspect relation with the will-planets—the Sun, Moon, Mercury, Venus, and Mars—reflect best the characteristics of the era. We will see in Volume XII, *Times to Come,* how perhaps the internalization of problems of the era, making them manifest in personal volition and causing "neuroses," carries with it *predictive significance for the age to come;* how the artist perhaps vents these tensions, these neuroses, and becomes a harbinger of future times. Problems are the vanguard of change.

It is not surprising that societal and generational influences internalized individually within the personal horoscope cause individual matrices of tension. That these tensions almost always affect one's manner of managing sexual energy and expressing love is perfectly reasonable: man must relate, must form relationships, must have another in order to see himself. For relationship he vents sexual energy, creativity, in many ways. When relationship is traumatic, there is isolation; apathy (the opposite of love) grows; moroseness and eventually self-destruction emerge; the "I" cannot exist without the "thou." In their expression of sex and love, love and sex, men and women are dependent upon each other within the society, the generation, the era, and within the prescriptions attached to these.

In the classical era, there were many words for love-sex: *agape* (ah-gah'-pay) was the feeling devoted to another's welfare, projected between persons, projected from God upon us all (called *caritas* by the Romans, from which we get the word *charity*); *philia* was friendship or brotherly love; *eros*, the drive to procreate manifested through desire to gain higher forms of being and relationship; *libido* was lust.

Today, the emphasis is different. Freud's theories have given great prominence to libido. Our present culture, perhaps in reaction to past prohibition and repression, and to the neuroses examined by Freud a generation ago, now tolerates open sexual expression. Eros is now used to dignify libido; philia and agape are confined to philosophical lectures in universities. The spectrum of love meanings has evolved in the present to an emphasis upon libido.

Perhaps this is a correspondence to the Uranus-Pluto square of 1931-35 (an intensification of self within the tensions of world perspective), the opposition between Neptune and Saturn of 1936-37 (a diffusion of ambition, a vague loss of personal direction), the conjunction of Saturn and Pluto during 1946-48 (refocus of the individual within world perspective, a sky's-the-limit philosophy, a reaction formation against earlier tensions), Neptune's transit through Libra, square Uranus, during 1951-56, and through Scorpio in 1957-70, while Pluto entered Libra

(1971). Through the Second World War and during post-war world reconstruction, the individual has gained a freedom never known before. Relationships are vitalized as never before. Expressivity, uniqueness, technology are all demanded by the booming society. New perspectives in love and marriage, in justice, in projections of the mind and spirit are all now internalized within new individuals in a new society. Sex—libido—is one of the energies affected. It is the energy now at a premium among the majority. Sex says "I am" more forcefully than any other kind of energy at present.

The astrologer must be aware of the tensions generated by the complex interrelationships between love and sex and by the cultural shift to a greater emphasis upon libido and eros.

Second: the technocracy of our times demands efficiency. In relationships, men and women must be efficient. Of course, this applies to financial management, home maintenance, job fulfillment, etc., and it also applies to the expression of sex and love. With the premium upon efficiency and the isolation of function from motivation (sex and love), the techniques of expressing sex gain enormous importance. The whispered question in another generation was "Will the person relate sexually?"; the question now is *"How well* does the person relate sexually?"

This emphasis on technique both liberates and ensnares. It presupposes and encourages openness and makes sexual expression a learnable skill. Both conditions take sex out of the closet, undoing the secrecy that sometimes resulted in distorted or frustrated behavior in the past, and thus may contribute to healthier sexual development. On the other hand, the emphasis on technique can confuse even further the relationship between sex and love. Hundreds of books now describe sexual techniques under the guise of the art of loving. Science has made a technical intrusion upon a field of art or spirit. Furthermore, being a good technician, performing well sexually, seems to many to guarantee the forming and maintaining of relationships.

Sexual performance has now become an index of social worth, personal integrity, and individual pride. But there are enormous pressures associated with the demand for performance. Studies show an increase in male impotence, for example, correlated with increased freedom of sexual expression for both men and women. The astrologer must recognize these pressures, be knowledgeable about qualified sexual therapy clinics as a possible remedy for some disfunctions, and be conscious of problems arising out of too great an emphasis upon technique.

Third: sex is the individual's most powerful intrinsic force. In many different ways it both creates life and destroys it. Wars are fought, relationships are made or broken, creations are brought to life for good or destruction. Society fears the full recognition and acknowledgment of such a powerful force. Unrestrained sexual expression can disrupt social mores, ordered family structure, and community organization.

Yet, repression of the force upsets other functions of the identity: the nervous system, the mind, ambition, the hope for reward, self-esteem, fantasy, world perspective. We must in mature perspective recognize this force and realize that giving it recognition does not mean we cannot control it.

These three philosophical areas of tension about sex—the sex-love relationship, technocratic emphasis upon efficiency, and social recognition of the powerful force—pervade every horoscope we study in this era. Even more, these considerations permeate *us,* the astrologers living within this era as individuals ourselves. In order to be of maximum service to our clients, we must acknowledge the sexuality dimension of our present time, and the sexuality dimension within each of us as individuals. Only then can we identify with the needs, tensions, and fulfillment potentials of others establishing relationships within the world.

For eighty to eighty-five percent of all female clients who come to me for astrological analysis, discussion of the sex profile revealed in the horoscope is important. These women of all ages, from fifteen to sixty-five (and a few isolated older cases), absorb the sexual pressures and expectancies embodied in our present time. There are pressures upon them to perform efficiently, to achieve orgasm easily; there is guilt about sexual expression now in relation to the rules set by parents in the past; there are anxieties about masturbation or the reliance upon it at the expense of the relationship or in reaction to sexual difficulties within it; there are tensions about promiscuity and abortion.

The percentage of men for whom the sexual profile is an essential part of astrological analysis seems much lower, perhaps thirty percent of my practice. The main concerns of the males seem to be homosexuality, premature ejaculation, management of anxiety within a sexually unsatisfying marital relationship, and promiscuity.

Astrology must address itself to the sex profile in terms of societal pressures in order to serve completely.

As soon as we study the horoscope for the sex profile, attention must be given first to the House V-XI axis. The Vth is associated with love-given and the XIth, with love-received. The Sign on the cusp of the Vth, the planet ruling the Sign on the Vth, and any planets placed within this House will immediately lead us further in our deductions. For example, Saturn in V in a woman's horoscope may suggest a sexual difficulty or dissatisfaction: a difficulty with conception or child bearing, even the use of sex as a strategy or weapon.

The planets—all of them—take on a sexual symbolism: Mercury suggests the mental view of sex, the nervous system within sexual tension; Venus, the affections, the social antennae; Mars, the actual sexual energy, the drive, the conquest, the reaction potential; Jupiter, the need for rewards in sexual experience, the religious dimension of sex, the philosophy about it; Saturn, the constriction of the sex drive, the discipline within it; Uranus, the accentuation of the self within the sex profile; Neptune, the suppression of the self within sexual reality; Pluto, the perspective brought to understanding and expressing sexuality. The Sun-Moon blend permeates the whole horoscope with its characteristic energy, translated into sexual terms.

Above all, the delineation of the sexual profile in a horoscope *demands recognition of the significance of sex in terms of relationships.* This focus then leads us to consider the parental factors, the upbringing. Then, immediately, we study the reactions of the mate and of friends, and the goals of the sexual energy in terms of the XIth; in fact, we can view the whole horoscope through derivative house readings, beginning with the VIIth as the other person's Ascendant. The whole horoscope speaks in terms of House-axes, ever stressing the concept of relationship, which is the goal of sexual energy.

Retrogradation becomes an extremely important symbolism. When a counterpoint is indicated through retrogradation among the planets Venus, Mars, and Jupiter, for example, there is immediately suggested a withdrawal, a reticence, a not-giving directly in terms of these planets' symbolism that affects the sex profile dramatically. There could be a difficulty in gaining fulfillment sexually (Venus retrograde), of applying sexual energy (Mars), of showing enthusiasm (Jupiter). With Saturn retrograde, there is the possibility of a legacy of inferiority feelings usually linked to the father or the father image in early life that certainly can affect the sex profile.

If the retrogradation symbolism falls within the Vth House or affects the ruler of the Vth, the reference to love and sex will be highly pronounced. The planets so involved often will rule the XIth, the VIIth, or part of the parental axis (X-IV), and the link between a problematic, tense, or obsessive sex profile and the love-sex attention received, the relationship dynamic, and parental influence is immediately obvious.

Hemisphere emphases become extremely telling as well, egocentrism (eastern hemisphere) can upset the relationship's balance; introversion (northern hemisphere) can work against full experience and expression; too much giving (western hemisphere), especially if it is taken advantage of, can imbalance relationships at the expense of the self-concept; victimization by experience (southern hemisphere) can destroy self-esteem.

Certain planets in certain Signs become important indices of sexual tension: Venus in Virgo suggests that the mind takes over the emotions, that cerebration displaces feeling, that acquaintances replace deep friendships, that understanding emotions displaces feeling them; Mars in Virgo suggests a passionate chastity or an objective detachment in sex. Venus in Capricorn suggests a delayed emotional development. Especially for the woman, Venus in Aries suggests the "tease," the ego working for its own benefit without sharing in relationships. In a man's horoscope, Venus in Aries can suggest misogamy or misogyny, the demeaning of marriage or women. Mars in Cancer in a woman's chart suggests that the native needs to rule the roost. Each astrologer must study the classic Planet-Sign meaning-image keys for application exclusively to the horoscope sex profile.

Certain aspects become very telling in sexual analysis: the square, opposition, or conjunction of Venus and Mars will suggest sex in high developmental focus in terms of the Sign and House references; the square, opposition, or conjunction between Venus and Saturn will suggest a confinement, a difficulty, an age discrepancy perhaps within the emotional expression; Venus in developmentally tense relationship with Uranus will intensify the emotions, and introduce innovation and adventure; with Neptune, the element of fantasy, drugs, deception; with Pluto, a potential waste of emotions, a hiding of them perhaps.

Mercury in developmental tension (square, opposition, or conjunction) with Mars or Uranus will heighten the nervous system strongly, directly affecting the neurological involvement with or need for the sexual act; with Neptune, the fantasy dimension will dominate; with Pluto, the perspective may lose reference to reality.

For the male, the aspect configuration involving his Moon will be extremely important in determining that part of his reigning need that is fulfilled through sexual relationship and thus his potential for emotional fulfillment with a woman. For the female, the aspect configuration involving her Sun will be more important, often involving her relationship with her father, the prime masculine symbol within her life.

The whole horoscope structure will speak through the level of sex-love, giving and receiving. Every tension, every need must be recognized at this level if a sexual problem is involved. Some examples will easily make these specific guidelines clear.

The woman's horoscope on page 88 shows the Sun in Pisces and the Moon in Virgo: there will be great discrimination in drawing upon the life-store of emotional intuition. The Scorpio Ascendant and the Grand Trine in Water among Venus, Jupiter, and Pluto (not involving the Sun or Moon) immediately suggest a strong emotional self-sufficiency, a separateness of her emotional "circuitry."

The ruler of the Vth, Neptune, is retrograde in the Xth. Jupiter, co-ruler of the Vth, is within the Grand Trine.

The Sun is in exact conjunction with Saturn in the IVth. Sexually, we sense an emotionally self-sufficient, a "loner" profile within the home. Venus within the Grand Trine is opposed the Moon, another indication of aesthetic awareness but perhaps also of an uncertainty, a separation from public experience in fear of failure. This deduction is extremely important because it links the Grand Trine with the Moon and because Venus rules Taurus on VII (relationship) and Libra on XII (limitations).

Mercury, ruler of the XIth (her husband's Vth) is retrograde on the cusp of the IVth.

We see this woman as emotionally self-sufficient, aesthetically self-pleasing, a loner within her own home, whose husband has withdrawn his affections somehow for some reason. Her position within the marriage, her point of honor (X), is "other than it seems" (Neptune, dispositor

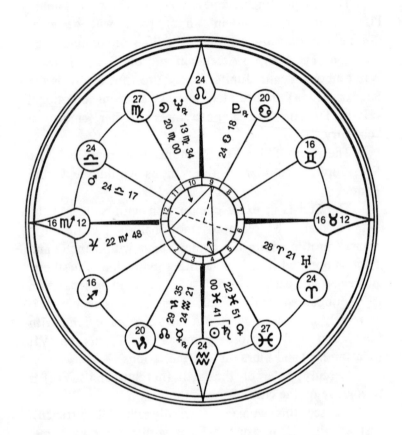

of Sun, Saturn, and Venus, placed in X, retrograde, conjunct the Moon and opposed the Sun). Her aesthetic relationship with her husband (Venus, ruler of Taurus on VII) is as far away as can be from her intellectualized formulation of her needs within the relationship (Moon in Virgo opposing Venus).

The major tension within the horoscope is within the T Cross among Mars-Uranus and Pluto. Pluto's retrogradation within the IXth (higher mind), its position as ruler of the Ascendant, within the Grand Trine and exactly quincunx retrograde Mercury, further corroborates all initial deductions. The T Cross keys us to repressed energy with Mars in XII and all three planets within Cadent (reactant) Houses. The woman holds back, does nothing to change the unfulfilled relationship with her husband.

Viewing this reservoir of energy, the T Cross, through derivative House technique, we begin to see much more of the concern: Uranus is in VI, the second of her Vth, her nervous anxiety about her sexual self-worth. This Uranus is in the twelfth of her VIIth, her husband's twelfth: her husband's individuality is somehow hidden or limited as well, his honor within the sexual profile (Uranus rules Aquarius on her IVth, his tenth). Pluto in her IXth is in his third; Pluto rules her Ascendant, his seventh (his wife): he can't communicate with her about sex, about her emotional self-sufficiency; its perspective (Pluto) is linked with his withdrawal of love and attention (quincunx with Mercury retrograde). His own sexuality (XI, his fifth) is running a counterpoint as well (Mercury retrograde on her IVth, his tenth).

Details pile upon details. When I simply mentioned to this woman that we had to talk about her sexual relationship with her husband, she replied, "There is none."

With the enormous self-containment within the horoscope that would keep her from giving freely, with the retrogradation points, the discriminating idealism, the anxiety about her own sexual performance, it was clear that sexually they simply could not communicate. It was clear that her inability to have orgasm during the sexual act had alienated her and her husband from each other. Within today's societal prescription, the female's orgasmic response determines the success of the sexual relationship. Without this response, the husband faced repeated feelings of failure. He could not take it any longer; she couldn't either; and both of them stopped having sexual contact.

The reservoir of energy in this horoscope is very powerful in strength (Cardinal Signs), reactant in experience (Cadent Houses). Pluto, ruler of the Ascendant and a direct symbol of sexuality, is also involved with the separatist emotional Grand Trine. It was clear that the woman released her sexual energies through masturbation: neurologically normal though maritally discordant with the need to fulfill relationship. The client corroborated these deductions completely.

When the horoscope is "turned around" to be read for the husband, he has the Water Grand Trine as well. In addition to being a valid astrological deduction, it is also a reasonable, common-sensical deduction: when one party within a relationship is emotionally self-sufficient, the other will have to be emotionally self-sufficient in order to keep the relationship together. It was disclosed within the interview that the husband had developed an isolated sexual life that was entirely masturbatory also.

Analysis proceeded toward the goal of bringing the two together out of their mutual isolation. Their high intelligence and education allowed uninhibited counsel. The great need on her part for intense stimulation to gain orgasm (T Cross) suggested counsel focused on technique and even surgical assistance. The technocracy had to be employed to help remedy the problems the technocracy itself had created.

In deep dialogue, it was clear that the woman's difficulty in relating, in giving herself with the freedom encouraged by her love for her husband, was indirectly traceable to a problem with the father (Saturn, co-ruler of Aquarius on IV, exactly conjunct the Sun, ruler of X). The woman said that her father "never existed," that he was completely out of the family picture. She had no male model visible for herself or within the relationship between her mother and father, which could enable her to understand love and sex within a relationship. Her emotional Grand Trine worked within her when she was a child too; Pluto within the IXth made her feel that she had all the answers with her highly developed intuition. Her discriminating personality then took her intuitions, her feelings, and filed them away. She existed alone in every

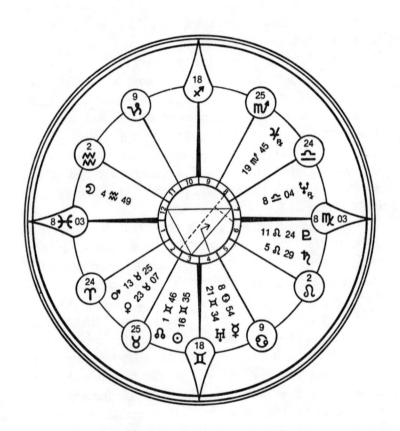

crowd and within her relationship. She was a take-charge woman (Moon in X) and ran things the way with which she was most comfortable, keeping her emotions to herself for solitary gratification.

The Sun-Moon blend of the woman whose horoscope appears on page 92 reveals a fine, facile intelligence, giving excellent expressivity, and a definite humanitarian outlook (Moon in Aquarius). Both the Sun and Moon, however, are within an Air Grand Trine involving Neptune retrograde in VII. With this Grand Trine placing the Moon in XII, we can assume a debilitation within the expressive personality, a confinement in fulfilling the reigning "people" needs represented by the Moon, which rules V.

The emphasis of the northern hemisphere corroborates a personality depression further. The only two planets above the horizon (Jupiter and Neptune) are both retrograde. Neptune rules the Ascendant and Jupiter rules the Midheaven, the point of highest self-esteem.

Mercury, dispositor of the Sun, is almost exactly square Neptune, introducing a daydreaming, perhaps romanticizing dimension (Mercury in Cancer) into the social and intellectual self-containment of the Air Grand Trine. Mercury rules the VIIth.

We know that Neptune within the VIIth suggests something other than what appears, here in terms of partner, mate, husband, relationship. The image of Neptune in the VIIth is a relationship dependent upon the native's support of the other party somehow. The extreme would be a marriage to someone in a wheelchair, requiring the supportive attention of the native.

Venus opposed Jupiter retrograde suggests a waste of emotional resources. The Moon opposes Saturn, ruler of IX, love received.

I suggested to the client that her relationships with men were continually supportive, somehow always helping out others with their problems (all Angles mutable). She agreed. I asked if perhaps some of her relationships had been with alcoholics (Neptune). She replied, "I seem to attract alcoholic, problematic men; my father was an alcoholic." The whole picture was clear: the young woman sacrificed herself totally to maintaining relationships dependent upon her support, defended herself through a romanticized, mental self-containment, and endured life, as she put it, "as a loner." At the time of analysis, she was deeply involved with a problematic male, but was living alone.

All these confinements of her potentially voluble and expressive personality depressed her sexually as well. She was unable to achieve orgasm through intercourse and only through highly romanticized fantasy during masturbation.

She related that her father was violent and pursued her sexually (Saturn semi-square the Sun, opposed the Moon; Uranus in IV conjunct the Sun; Mercury, ruler of the IVth, square Neptune within the Grand Trine and in VII). She added that she had taken on a deep inferiority about her beauty from her mother (Jupiter, ruler of X, retrograde and opposed Mars, ruler of II, self-worth, and opposed Venus).

The horoscope on page 96 is that of a male politician.

With the Sun in Taurus and the Moon in Capricorn, there would be a yearning for administrative influence. Idealism and realism would work hand in hand to create a materialistic structure. Controlling his own security would have been the goal of his life. This grand, organized thrust certainly involves the public (Sun in VII) and a flow of information or propaganda that would be enormous (Moon conjunct Jupiter in III, Jupiter ruling Sagittarius on III). Saturn in Leo in X corroborates the scope of ambition even further.

But there are problems that are definitely sexual: Venus is retrograde (ruler of the Ascendant) and exactly conjunct Mars, and both Venus and Mars square the elevated Saturn. There are no "points" in water: the emotions would have no frame of reference. Emotional projection would seek identification with some movement, some lofty principle in order to gain definition. With the emotions (Venus) under such duress (conjunction with Mars, square with Saturn), the projection would be traumatic, linked to an enormous bureaucratic ambition (Moon in Capricorn, elevated Saturn in Leo).

Neptune rules the Vth and is in conjunction with Pluto in the VIIIth. The emotional fantasy would easily be projected out of perspective. Mercury is dispositor of both Pluto and Neptune and opposes Uranus upon the horizon. The nervous system would be totally involved within the emotional trauma and its projection upon the public.

This is Adolf Hitler's horoscope. Psychoanalytically, the root of the problems is surely his relationship with his parents (Leo, Aquarius): Uranus-Saturn and the Sun are

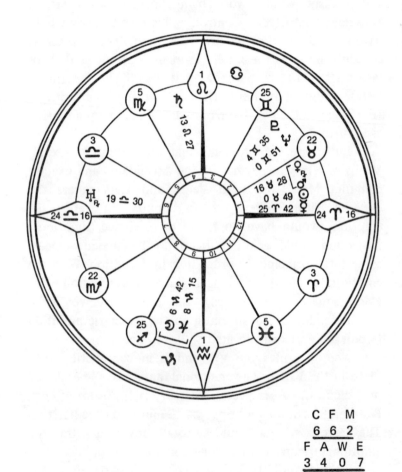

```
C F M
6 6 2
F A W E
3 4 0 7
```

involved within the enormous tension constructs. Much has been written about Hitler's heterosexual masochism (the afflictions to Venus) and his reaction formation that transferred, projected his maniacal (perverted genius, Uranus at the Ascendant) frustrations upon the public (the Germans as well as the Jews; VIII, other peoples' worth). The major developmental crises in Hitler's personality surely occurred around his thirteenth year: Solar-Arc progression of the Moon to square Uranus, progressed Sun to square Saturn.

The man's horoscope which appears on page 98 shows a decidedly eastern hemisphere orientation. We immediately begin to anticipate egocentrism. The Sun and Moon are both in Cancer: sensitivity and self-protection will gain tremendous emphasis. The emotions will become a shelter against the intrusion of the world. High-level affections and great values will be sought within the security of the home and among friends. Cautious and sensitive approaches will be learned through emotionally trying experiences. Loneliness will be easily accepted to avoid hurt by the world. This core delineation is supported further by the position of the Sun and Moon in the XIth (love received), square Neptune in II (self-worth).

Venus is retrograde, suggesting an emotional counterpoint, perhaps a cerebrated (Gemini) emotional self-indulgence. In conjunction with Uranus, the intellectualized emotional inversion gains a tremendous accentuation of ego. Additionally, Mercury, ruler of the Ascendant and Midheaven, is stationary-direct within the

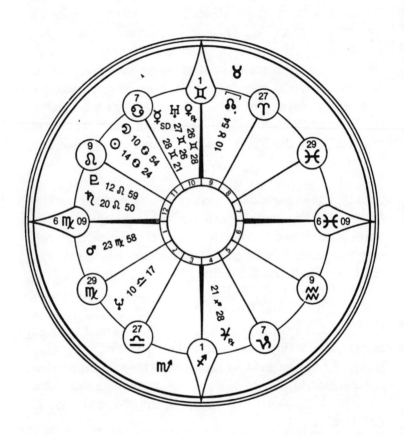

Uranus-Venus conjunction and focuses the entire being upon intensifying the ego's needs for personal emotional security. This triple conjunction is square Mars in Virgo within the Ascendant: the tension will be great, to the point of making the native finical.

Externalization in relationships will be difficult since Neptune, ruler of Pisces on the VIIth, is exactly square the Moon (and the Sun). The element of fantasy about ego worth and love received will be a dominant theme within the life development. Jupiter's opposition to the triple conjunction in X will expand the emotional anxiety and self-intensification greatly and key us to the root cause within the parental influence, since Mercury and Jupiter rule the parental axis (Gemini and Sagittarius, X-IV) and are in opposition.

Saturn rules Capricorn on the Vth (often sex for the sake of sex, down-to-earth romantic profile) and is within the XIIth, suggesting that this young man's ambition for emotional fulfillment needs the leadership of someone else, someone to work with him in achieving the ego's need for emotional security (Saturn in Leo). Saturn is conjunct Pluto, the conjunction that places him within the generation born shortly after the end of the war, the generation which, in early expression of personal ambition, seeks to rebel and recondition society, with the means of rebellion becoming more important and more clear than its end.

There is no doubt about it: this male, through every measurement *translated into behavior,* is a homosexual.

The female whose horoscope appears on page 100 said

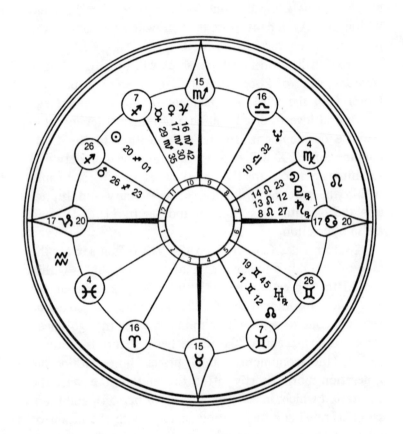

that her reason for having her horoscope analyzed was to assist in a relocation decision. But quick inspection of the sex profile, the relationship index, reveals that there is a great deal more to her decision.

The first clue is the retrogradation of Saturn (ruler of the Ascendant) and Pluto (ruler of the Midheaven) within the VIIth, the House of relationships. The VIIth is ruled by the Moon, also in the VIIth, and the Sun, dispositor of the Moon in opposition with Uranus in the Vth, retrograde. The Sun within this tense opposition is in the XIth: love-received.

The VIIth House is withdrawn (the retrogradation and the interception) and under tension (rulers' aspects). The tension is very strong, perhaps locked within the personality, since the VIIth House group is squared by the Xth House group, both groups in Angles and Fixed Signs. Venus in conjunction with Jupiter in Scorpio at the Midheaven suggests strongly that there is a deep sexual tension within relationships that continually makes them difficult and unsatisfying, that invites emotional waste (Venus square Pluto) or clandestine emotional activity. The tension undoubtedly stems from a fear of losing the independence (Sun opposed Uranus) which protects a legacy of inferiority feelings (Sun trine the VIIth House group).

The woman is definitely a person on public display (Moon in Leo in VII). The contradiction reveals the tension: a person within the public eye having great difficulty establishing relationships because of timidity and

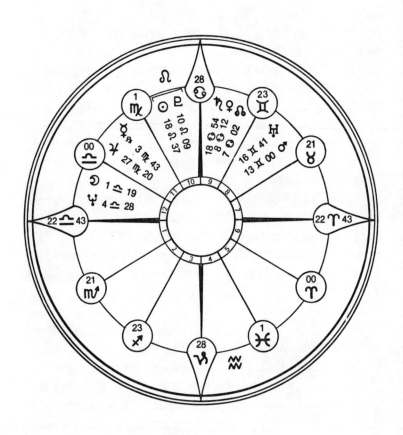

a sense of inferiority, traceable to parental influence (Venus and Pluto, parental rulers here, in square).

Upon my presentation of these deductions, this attractive airline stewardess opened up. Her problem with relocation involved a male and her fear of losing her independence (which meant a fear of confronting her problems head on, on a permanent basis). She was "afraid of getting stuck" (being unable to escape relationship tensions that occurred throughout her adult life). She said her father never gave her any personal endorsement (Saturn retrograde) and that her mother was "extremely possessive" (Pluto conjunction with the Moon, square the Venus-Jupiter conjunction).

Sexually symptomatic, she is unable to have orgasm in a relationship: she is fulfilled only through masturbation, requiring intense stimulation (Uranus in V) to unlock the rigid anxiety structure (X-VII square configuration in Fixed Signs). There were many other details that were relevant to the full analysis, based upon Mercury ruling Gemini on V, trine Saturn; IInd House ruler, Neptune, in VIII (ruled by Mercury) sextile the Sun, trine Uranus; and Venus square Pluto.

At first glance, the male's horoscope appearing on page 102 reveals a complete emphasis on the southern hemisphere: the self is thrown totally into experiences, running the risk of victimization and exploitation. The Sun in Leo and the Moon in Libra suggest that independence will gain romantic outlets in society, perhaps in an unusual personal philosophy. We would expect a strong, attractive dramatic flair. With Pluto oriental, we gain a corroboration of these deductions. With the Moon conjunct Neptune in XII, the Moon ruling the Midheaven, the Libra Ascendant, the Moon's mutual reception with Venus, Neptune ruling V, we are aware of the potential to be a musician, or a person somehow behind the scenes (Moon in XII) of a public musical presentation. The man is an arranger, director, and performer within a group appearing on the night-club circuit.

The man is keenly cerebral: Mars-Uranus conjunction in Gemini, Mercury and Jupiter in Virgo. His vocational goal is to be a show critic, a show "doctor," making adjustments objectively to improve musical acts presented to the public.

The sex profile becomes very important in the life of this man using creativity totally to earn his living. Neptune ruling the Vth in conjunction with the Moon in XII suggests a behind-the-scenes limitation, perhaps sexual. Venus in Cancer squares the Moon and Neptune in Libra and provides another corroboration. There would be a theatrical charade within the sex profile. The man is a homosexual.

The Moon becomes especially important here as a ruler of Cancer on the parental axis. It is square Venus, ruler of the Ascendant, and this Venus is conjunct the Moon's nodal axis, suggesting the strong influence of the mother, relating her to the sexual profile. The native corroborated that his mother was suffocatingly overprotective to the point that, as a youth, he was obese (Cancer emphasis). His father rejected him (Venus applying to Saturn, which is ruler of Capricorn on IV and exactly semi-square to Mercury in XI).

When transiting Saturn crossed the fourth cusp and Uranus transited Mercury, the father voiced rejection of the "mamma's boy." Six years later, when Saturn opposed the Moon-Neptune conjunction, the native had his first homosexual experience with a professional music teacher who was thirty years older than he (Saturn).

Now, no longer obese, free of parental influence, successful in his job, there is no concern or anxiety about homosexuality. The horoscope analysis turned to other concerns.

The male's horoscope on page 106 suggests a difficult challenge to the identity. The Sun in Aries and the Moon in Gemini promise a heated information flow that can be excessive, a diversity and curiosity that might create difficulties in establishing long-range focus. We note that there is no opposition within the horoscope; focus will be difficult.

The Sun is in the VIIIth, in conjunction with Saturn: the Aries energy will be hidden perhaps (Sun rules XII), hard to reach—for the native and for others in response to him. The Moon in IX suggests that the individuality will lose significance in the context of the philosophies and communications of others. This will be difficult for the Aries life-energy to take. With this energy itself "undercover" in the VIIIth, within a conjunction with Saturn, we see that there definitely will be a problem, a challenge to externalization. Saturn rules Capricorn on the

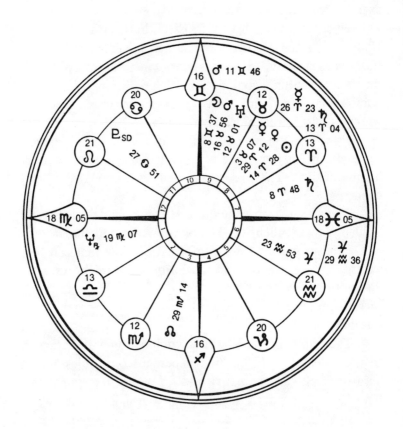

Vth and the Moon rules Cancer on the XIth: the concern will have part of its manifestation in affairs of love and sex.

Venus is in Aries, suggesting that this male will have highly intensified sexual and emotional feelings, perhaps will express a fear or contempt of women. These feelings will be covered over too, in tension, since Venus is also in VIII and square to Pluto in XI. Pluto is the only "point" in Water; the man's emotional perspective is indeed vague, is within a tense frame of reference.

The Moon is square to the rising Neptune (only Neptune and Saturn are in Angles). The tension of fantasy, dreams, substitution, camouflage enters into the whole problem situation as it is developing in our deductions. The only major supportive aspects within the horoscope are the trines made by Mars and Uranus to this Neptune. The deduction was easy and was corroborated by the client: intensive masturbation and fantasy had served to ease, to sedate sex tensions, and then alcoholism developed for the same purpose. All relationships were made through substitution of masturbation for liaison, fantasy for actuality, ego camouflage through alcoholism for direct ego presentation (Neptune rules Pisces on VII). At thirty-six, this male was *not* a homosexual, was single, and was still a virgin.

The Sun-Saturn conjunction was corroborated by his admission that he is a "loner" but "wants desperately to be recognized as an authority." Investigation into the friction or upset with the father (Jupiter, ruler of IV, semi-square Saturn) revealed that his father had a hot temper, was revered by the public as a state representative, but was not respected by the family. As a business executive involved in managing the efficiency of others' research work (Moon in IX; Mercury ruler of Ascendant and Midheaven), the native said his goal was "to be business-like instead of loving."

The approaching square between Mars and Jupiter—an extremely important aspect in any horoscope—connotes the gambler, expansive energies and self-assurance, impulsiveness requiring moderation. Often, this aspect accompanies intense disruption of societal standards. This was the native's motivation to seek astrological guidance: he had a job-history of disruption, firings, rehirings, being thrown out (Jupiter in VI; Mars, dispositor of Sun and Saturn, ruler of VIII, co-ruler of III). At the time of his horoscope appointment, progressed Saturn was upon his Sun, progressed Mars was just leaving conjunction with the Moon, and progressed Jupiter was squaring the nodal axis.

Here was the man deeply troubled emotionally with unfulfillment, talented in his job yet extremely disruptive, out of focus emotionally and vocationally; deeply frustrated with an unformed personal perspective.

Mercury rules the Midheaven and the Ascendant and is the dispositor of the Moon and Neptune. Mercury is in conjunction with Venus across the Sign-line, indicating a tremendous emotional idealism attached to his potential for self-projection. Mercury is applying to a conjunction with Uranus. Through dialogue, it became clear that he hated himself for all his emotional problems with a world and peer group that were having anything *but* sexual problems! He hated himself (his words) because he hadn't met his own idealistic standards. This was a powerful admission on his part and was the central theme of the horoscope analysis.

His fear of loving others (the Venus-Pluto configuration, VIII-XI) had to be solved by his learning to appreciate himself first. Together, we followed the strength of his Mercury (separating from a square with Pluto, another reference to imbalanced personal perspective), through its period of progressed retrogradation between the ages seven and thirty-one, into its direct development in conjunction with radical Venus within the next five years. At the time of consultation, the progressed Mercury *was* squaring the radical Pluto in XI, a time for the final alteration of perspective in his life, perhaps; a time when this whole situation could be cleared up.

He said he never thought much about going to a prostitute (Venus square Pluto) because that would degrade him further. He had stopped asking girls out on dates because he was afraid of being turned down (Aries pride). Strangely, but understandably within the Mercury symbolism, the Ascendant, and Neptune particularly, he said that he became erotically excited whenever he was in a library or an art museum. The subject matter was unimportant in these places, but the accumulation of knowledge, perhaps the idealization of all knowledge, excited him sexually. The analysis then pursued his grand interests in art, music (Neptune), reading (Mercury), foreign languages (IXth House), etc. Behaviorally, a conjunction *within behavioral development* was developed between these Mercury interests, personal ideals, and heterosexual relationship potentials. Humorously simplified as it may appear, the joining of the two had never been thought of by the native: to take a girl with the same interests to a library or a museum, to read a book together! The man had never thought of this, since his emotional perspectives (Pluto) were caught up with those of his "buddies," his many roommates, his friends (Pluto in XI). His fantasies were being conditioned by *their* ideals and not his own. The emotional perspective was now undergoing new alteration so that he could focus upon what he needed for himself. Venus within the configuration rules II, self-worth. Appreciating himself and his own needs clearly would help introduce secure love into his emotional and business lives.

Except for Hitler, the six other individuals whose horoscopes appear in the preceding examples live as so-called "perfectly normal, average, ordinary, routine people." This is the only value judgment that has been made, and as an objective astrologer I am uncomfortable making even this judgment. The point *must* be made, however, that there is nothing sensational or extraordinarily problematic about any one of the six examples. It is a testament to the infinite complexity of life that each life contains within it networks of interrelated need tensions with different foci, the sum total of which determines identity. At the same time, to have ignored these particularly sexually oriented need networks would have been to miss the entire focus of the tension—*and the direction of counsel and guidance.*

There are astrologers who, when serving a homosexual client, for example, will try to "cure" his or her homosexuality, when many homosexuals these days feel "comfortable" with their choice or inclination. Society has allowed the expression which, in times past, was repressed and became a problematic tension. Such moralizing represents an irresponsible personal intrusion by the astrologer. Granted, should a client come to the astrologer with a concern about homosexuality that *is* problematic, that motivated the appointment for analysis, the astrologer must do all that is possible, based upon his or her study within the field, to assist the client to solve the problem. The two major strengths we have as astrologers in situations which are seriously problematic, which disrupt life flow and relationships severely, are knowledge of other fields besides Astrology and the sense to refer the client to medical, psychological, or spiritual specialists. Perhaps the ultimate service resource is for the astrologer to have a cooperative liaison with other specialists, which ideally will work both ways in analytical service to the client.

The example on page 112 is definitely severely problematic. The male has the Sun in Capricorn and the Moon in Libra: an administrative show would seem to have belied the need for social support. A prima-donna detachment would have evolved. He would have the need to compromise somehow within the drive to be

Transits, progressions for surgery

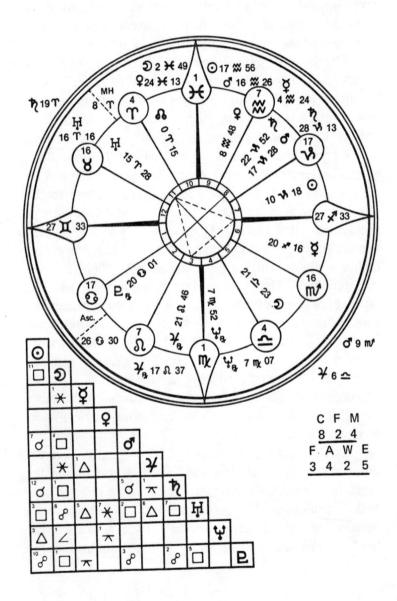

"masculine" (Sun) and the drive to be "feminine."

This cross-purpose is corroborated through the Grand Cross in Cardinal Signs: Moon opposed Uranus, and Pluto opposed Sun-Mars-Saturn. The detachment is corroborated through the Grand Trine in Fire among Uranus, Jupiter, and Mercury (not involving the Sun or Moon directly). The Grand Trine is diffused throughout the whole personality through the Moon's opposition with Uranus and its very close sextile with Jupiter in Leo and with Mercury. The Moon is enormously focused within Libra in the Vth House, ruling Cancer in II, self-worth.

The cross-purposes, the anxieties would have been extreme, undoubtedly bringing the "Cinderella complex" potential out of the Libran Moon. The focus was definitely upon the love-sex axis. The mutability of the Signs on all the Angles and the double-bodied Signs on the Midheaven and Ascendant further corroborated all these deductions. This is not simple bi-sexuality; it must be much more, an all-consuming trauma of sexual identity.

The co-rulers of the Midheaven are both retrograde (Jupiter and Neptune). Jupiter in Leo is correlated with a search for individual admiration more than anything else as a reward, and the retrogradation suggests a counterpoint in his communication (III) within relationships (ruler of VII). This symbolism would be very powerful through the almost exact sextile with the Libran Moon in V.

The Moon is further stressed through the squares with Mars, Saturn, and Pluto within the Grand Cross, the opposition with Uranus. We're back to where we began our deductions. The crisis for this male is undeniably a sexual identity trauma. It prompted him to enter the hospital and, through surgery, to achieve a sex-change. The progressions shown around the natal horoscope are for the month of the operation.

The progressed New Moon had occurred sixteen months earlier, just four months before his acceptance for deep preliminary psychological examinations in the trans-sexual clinic. At the time of the operation, the progressed Midheaven was squaring the Sun, sextiling Venus, and quincunxing Neptune; the progressed Sun and progressed Mars were in conjunction, sextile natal Uranus and opposed progressed Jupiter. *The progressed Moon was precisely conjunct the Midheaven.*

The major transits at the time of the operation were Saturn opposing Moon, Mars squaring Venus, Jupiter applying to conjunction transit of the natal Moon. This was the time of his/her life.

After the operation and careful post-surgical therapy, she returned to a new life, became manager of a woman's hair-styling salon. The cross-tensions were resolved; a proud exhibitionism remained. As the progressed Moon crossed natal Uranus, trined Jupiter, opposed its own natal position, squared Saturn, and sextiled the Ascendant all from the XIth House, she married. Saturn in transit was exactly upon the Ascendant; Uranus in transit was exactly upon the Moon in V; Jupiter was exactly upon Venus in IX, and Mars was upon the progressed Moon in XI.

Imagine the difficulties this identity crisis would have caused in an earlier generation. Society today—for better or worse, it makes no difference in this objective analysis–does allow sexual anomalies, freedom, help, adjustment, and expression. Perspectives have changed. For another example of change, there are astrological and medical books that show gruesome pictures of people supposedly totally devastated by the "secret vice," by "self-pollution," by masturbation. Yet, other cultures refer to masturbation as "enjoying one's self" (*Selbstbefriedigung*). Today masturbation can even be reasonably *prescribed* to help a person appreciate personal sexual potential, to help along a lagging sexual development. Times have changed: they bring new freedoms, and, as with freedoms of any kind, there are responsibilities, comforts, disciplines, guilts, fulfillments, and escapes to be reckoned with.

The astrologer is not a moralist. He or she blends needs with reality through relationships within time. This is the expert astrologer's freedom. The discipline and responsibility, the comfort and fulfillment within this freedom begin with knowing one's self.

Synastry

The whole of life depends upon success within relationships: the relationship of the individual with the natural, human, and material environment, his relationship with internal psychological, neurological, chemical, and spiritual dimensions. The concept of needs catalyzes all these relationships; need tensions arise, seeking fulfillment to bring comfort to the individual system. Only in death is the system free of need tension (Volume V).

Synastry is the word for astrological chart

comparison, indicating the relationship between two individuals, the reciprocal alinement of two astrological configurations, the interaction between two complex systems of needs, two identities. Relationships of all kinds fall within synastry: marriage relationships, work relationships, fatalistic relationships, etc. Two horoscopes meet, intertwine, create extra tensions, bring extra comforts.

Comparison must begin between the Suns and Moons of both horoscopes: trines will suggest a definite ease, support, and harmony; squares or oppositions will introduce developmental tensions; conjunctions will suggest a great unity of focus but perhaps not allow enough developmental tension for growth together. Even in the face of strong disparate tensions, the trine of the Suns will make overall compatibility possible, probable. In essence, the Sun-Moon blend of both horoscopes must be studied together with the support, tension, or focal points isolated for detailed study, guided by the cross-aspects between the two charts. Wide orbs can be allowed with the lights in synastry, concentrating heavily upon elemental emphasis. Of course, the closer the aspect the more pronounced will be the relationship factors revealed by the analysis.

When the Suns or Moons make no aspect with each other, the concentration is upon the individual Sun-Moon blends and the elemental compatibility; then, the focus shifts to the House positions of one person's Sun and Moon in the other person's chart. The Sun of one in the XIIth of the other certainly would suggest confinement of the former by the latter, a sense of limitation perhaps, unless there were an unusually fine aspect relationship involved as well. The Moon comparisons should be interpreted in terms of one person's needs (Volume V) within the other's field of experience, shown by the new House placement within the comparison.

The next step involves comparison of the planetary positions: the Mercurys' relationships by Sign, aspect, and House will show the quality of the synastric "meeting of the minds"; the Venus' relationships will suggest the emotional compatibility; the relationships between the Mars will show the energy interrelationships, perhaps the sexual vigor; between the Jupiters, the hopes for reward and enthusiasm in the relationship; between the Saturns, alinement of individual ambitions; Uranus comparisons will suggest the cooperation of individual self-concepts, in what experiences of one person the other's intensification of self-awareness will be registered; the Neptunes will aline the fantasies, the potential deceptions; the Plutos will suggest important points of perspective that will blend to place the diadic relationship within world relationship.[1]

The final step in comparison involves aspects made between the planets, one horoscope to the other. *Against the background of full analysis of each of the two charts done beforehand,* the aspect interrelationships become dynamic networks of one person's need-tension matrix

---

1. Usually, the trans-Saturnian planets in both horoscopes will be in the same Sign because of nearness in age in relation to the slowness of the planets in orbit. Then, the House relationship is extremely important. If the Signs *are* different, the Sign variable becomes important indeed, as does the probable age or generation difference.

Eva Braun

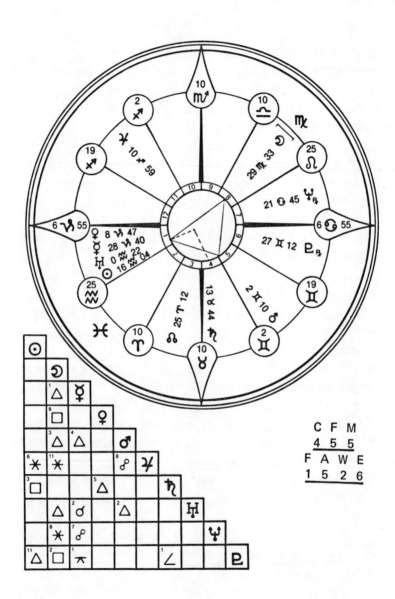

C F M
4 5 5
F A W E
1 5 2 6

reacting with that of the other. The positions by Sign, House, and the aspect of the Ascendant and Midheaven must also be noted. A very obvious and important example is when the Saturn of one horoscope falls upon the Ascendant of the other: the former's ambition will totally dominate the self-projection of the latter.

A very important specific point is when the planet of one horoscope falls upon the *south* lunar node (℧) of the other horoscope: the tendency is for the former to drain the latter, to expolit, lead on, use up the latter. This is a powerfully debilitating synastric correspondence; the more significantly emphasized the planet within the axis conjunction, the more dramatic the usurpation.

After the astrological concommitants are deduced, common sense must take over. A relationship portrait in terms of needs and behavior, support and tension, individuality and cooperation emerges. Tension must be present to maintain growth and interest; ease must be present to preserve comfort and achievement.

The first example is the horoscope comparison between Adolf Hitler and his "mistress," Eva Braun.

Eva Braun's Moon was void of course, only 27 minutes of arc away from entering Libra (page 118). The orbs of its trine aspects with Uranus and Mars are very close, bringing the symbolism of the Moon much into Libra, into a closed circuit (Grand Trine) of social and intellectual self-sufficiency. This is corroborated by the Moon's "hidden" position, its interception within the VIIIth House. The Sun-Moon blend would have to include the Moon's significances in Virgo *and* Libra, reflecting the

Sun in Aquarius: the mental closed circuit would be a definite asset, possibly used defensively (Moon's House position). The emotions would be bound up with the thinking process (Virgo). The social and the romantic would rise in importance and perhaps threaten the system. The self's highly valued sense of loyalty would probably have difficulty standing strong against the duplicity of others. Tolerance and sympathy would be learned. The tendency would be to give up making a personal mark since ease within the status quo, within the society, would be so easily attained—i.e., the defense would work so well—that persistent effort would be diluted.

The squares to the Moon by Venus and Pluto would corroborate these initial deductions and carry them further: personal perspective, the press upon personal needs, the desire to be thought intelligent, to be accepted socially would all be under strong tension. Her reputation, her point of honor would be under tense development (Pluto rules the Midheaven).

The nerves would be under stress within this urge to project the self uniquely (Mercury conjunct Uranus in Aquarius in the Ascendant with the Sun and also within the Grand Trine; Mercury rules Gemini on VI and is dispositor of the Moon). There would be parental tensions, probably with the father, that would follow her in development and be projected upon other men in her life as well: Sun square Saturn in IV; Venus, ruler of IV, and Saturn, ruler of the Ascendant, in mutual reception; Venus square the Moon; Pluto, ruler of X, in square with the Moon.

The Moon rules Cancer on VII: relationships.

Neptune is within VII and is retrograde. This timid, socially defensive woman would somehow change the perspective of her life through a unique social emergence, upsetting her family, that would involve her tolerances, sympathies, and support. Her relationships with a mate would be other than they seemed. Perhaps they would be endured within a state of romantic daydreaming, nervous fantasy, sublimated hopes (Mercury opposed Neptune; Mercury ruling V, Neptune ruling Pisces in II, self-worth). Her own emotional frame of reference would be vague: only the Midheaven and Neptune are in Water Signs. Lastly, Venus rising at the Ascendant is in Capricorn, suggesting a delayed emotional development, especially square the Moon even though trine Saturn. An older man perhaps would be the one to supplant the father, alter her perspective (Saturn semi-square Pluto, ruler of the Midheaven), and possess her in isolation or confinement (Moon interception in VIII, the second of the VIIth).

This sketch of Eva Braun's horoscope is corroborated by Albert Speer in *Inside the Third Reich* (London: Weidenfeld and Nicolson, 1970; pp. 92-93):

Eva Braun came of a family of modest circumstances . . . [she] remained simple . . . had no interest in politics. She scarcely ever attempted to influence Hitler. With a good eye for the facts of everyday life, however, she did sometimes make remarks about minor abuses in conditions in Munich. She was sports loving, a good skier with plenty of endurance.

Eva Braun was allowed to be present during visits from old party associates. She was banished as soon as other dignitaries of the Reich appeared at the table. Even when Goering and his wife came, Eva Braun had to stay in her room. Hitler obviously regarded her as socially acceptable within strict limits. Sometimes I kept her company in her exile, a room next to Hitler's bedroom. She was so intimidated that she did not dare leave the house for a walk. . . . In general Hitler showed little consideration for her feelings. He would enlarge on his attitude toward women as though she were not present: 'A highly intelligent man should take a primitive and stupid woman. Imagine if on top of everything else I had a woman who interfered with my work! In my leisure time I want to have peace . . . I could never marry.'

Then, on page 46:

I could only wonder at the way Hitler and Eva Braun avoided anything that might suggest an intimate relationship.

On page 101:

Even toward Eva Braun he was never completely relaxed and human. The gulf between the leader of the nation and the simple girl was always maintained. Now and then, and it always struck a faintly jarring note, he would call her *Tschapperl*, a Bavarian peasant pet name with a slightly contemptuous flavor.

Eva Braun was anything but dumb: Mercury in Capricorn, within the Ascendant, dispositor of the Moon, trine the Moon; dispositor of Mars and trine Mars; conjunct Uranus; dispositor of Pluto and quincunx Pluto: the Moon's diurnal motion on her birthday was 14°04'. She was simple, "everyday," immature perhaps: Capricorn Ascendant, heavy Earth emphasis at the expense of Fire and Water; Venus in Capricorn.

Further corroboration is provided by William L. Shirer in *The Rise and Fall of the Third Reich* (New York: Simon and Schuster, 1960; p. 1111):

The daughter of lower-middle-class Bavarian peasants, who at first strenuously opposed her illicit relation with Hitler, even though he was the dictator . . . Eva, though installed in a suite in Hitler's Alpine villa, couldn't endure the long separations when he was away and twice tried to kill herself in the early years of their friendship. But gradually she accepted her frustrating and ambiguous rule—acknowledged neither as wife nor as mistress—content to be sole woman companion of the great man and making the most of their rare moments together. . . . It is obvious that his influence on her, as on so many others, was total.

Eva Braun: natal horoscope
Outer ring: Hitler natal horoscope

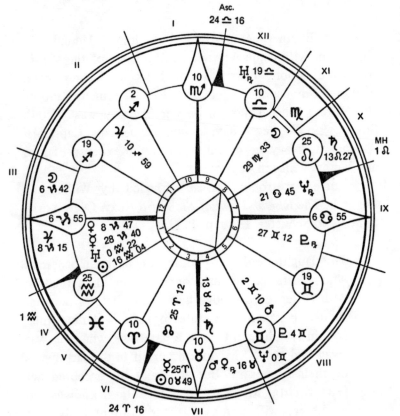

Hitler *possessed* Eva Braun for more than twelve years. Comparison of their horoscopes shows this possession dramatically (page 124).

Hitler's Moon was only thirteen minutes of arc from exact conjunction with Eva Braun's Ascendant: *he* was to become *her* personal projection of self. This is further suggested by Hitler's horizon and powerful nervous distortion (Mercury opposed Uranus) conjunct Eva Braun's nodal axis, only fifty-six minutes of arc from exactness. These two points of comparison are corroborated definitely by Hitler's Midheaven opposition to her Uranus with less than one-degree arc of exactness. This Uranus is Eva Braun's key point within the Grand Trine; her entire personality, individuality, and self-projection were usurped by Hitler.

Even taken further, the comparisons are startling: Hitler's Saturn opposes her Sun; and this Saturn squares her Saturn with only seventeen minutes of arc to partile.

Hitler's extremely debilitating conjunction of Venus retrograde and Mars falls upon Eva Braun's Saturn, this conjunction square Saturn in his own chart. It seems, in comparison, that the sexual and emotional distortions were somehow fulfilled in his relationship with Eva Braun. Further corroboration is seen in Hitler's Neptune-Pluto conjunction falling upon her Mars within her Grand Trine (Mars in V).

In the light of this possession, only two aspects kept life peaceful: Eva Braun's Sun trine Hitler's Uranus; Hitler's Jupiter almost exactly conjunct her Venus.

That there were tensions between them always,

Queen Elizabeth II of England

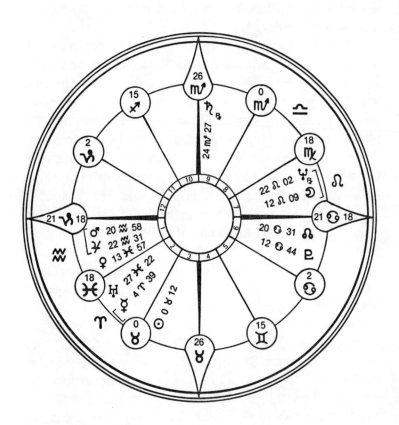

Prince Philip
Duke of Edinburgh

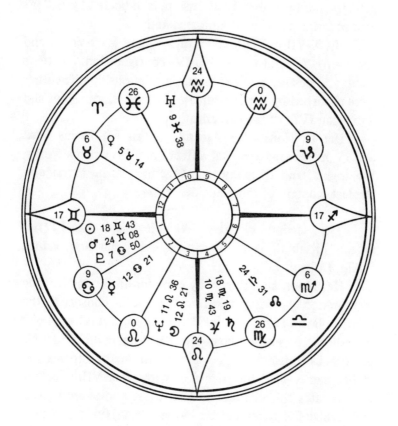

through frequent separations, causing her alleged suicide attempts early in their relationship, is indicated by Hitler's Sun squaring *her* Uranus almost exactly.

His X-VII difficulties (Saturn square Mars-Venus and the Sun) fall into her VII-IV configuration: Hitler's traumatic destiny and problematic relationship difficulties were absorbed by her Neptunian VIIth of relationships and Saturnian IVth of life's finalization.

Her Ist House, her Ascendant, fell within his IIIrd and IVth: perhaps her total reflection of his written works, his dogma, and their mystical togetherness in marriage in the last moment of joint suicide.

The second synastry example (pages 126-127) is Queen Elizabeth II of England and her husband, Prince Philip, Duke of Edinburgh.

Her Moon almost exactly conjoins his Moon-Neptune conjunction: he easily takes on the role of consort to the queen, plays the royal role. Her Moon in VII is her public figurehead, pageantry position. His Moon in the IIIrd is his position as emissary, go-between, distributor of information in her name. That his IIIrd falls within her VIIth further corroborates this deduction. That these bodies are in Leo and involve the symbol of the Moon (queen) further focuses the relationship between the royal pair.

With her Mercury square his Pluto, there probably is tension within his role. It probably took a lot of getting used to: his work on her behalf, following her directives within the roles they share, the roles she leads. Her

Capricorn Ascendant would help her very much in her administrative posture. It is much stronger than his Gemini Ascendant.

At the same time, her Venus trines his Pluto and would do much to soften whatever perspective tensions they had between them in the role-playing. His Neptune upon her Moon suggests that it is very easy for him to say just what she wants to hear, to keep her happy by doing just the right thing (his Neptune in III; her Moon in VII).

Her Jupiter—inheritance—crowns his Midheaven. His Venus is conjunct her Sun (five-degree orb).

There is still a strong tension within the relationship that will be hard to soften: his Mars squares her Uranus. His many varied interests (international horse shows, natural science expeditions) probably upset her, perhaps because of the money he spends (her IInd).

The key to synastric analysis in this marriage is certainly the conjunction of the Moons and the resulting conjunction of his Cadent IIIrd House with her Angular VIIth, the House of the public, the people she serves, whom they serve together.

Progressions and transits within the synastry of two horoscopes are very telling: an important development within one horoscope will involve the synastric point of the other. Together in relationship, one helps the other through tension and growth in ways revealed by the comparisons; one enjoys the other's success and development.

Fertility

The hoped-for product of heterosexual relationship is offspring. Having children is the basic goal of sexual energy. Although ancient astrological discoveries dealt with fertility, it is only now that these discoveries have been reinforced by scientific testing and are heralded in terms of the technocracy: "birth control through astrology."

Dr. Eugen Jonas, a Czechoslovakian psychiatrist, astrological researcher, and computer scientist, conducted many control experiments for almost a decade, exploring birth-control cycles known long ago to astrologers. He statistically proved that a woman has *two* fertility cycles each month: the regular ovulation cycle (the medical cycle) and an astrological cycle. His works claim a ninety-eight percent effective rate in controlling birth (conception), and sex selection (boy or girl) when a child was desired.

The premise is extremely simple. It waited centuries until the computer and modern perspectives on sex would allow comprehensive testing procedures. *A woman is fertile within the astrological cycle when the Sun and Moon in transit every month make the same angular (aspect) relationship that exists between the Sun and Moon in the woman's birth horoscope. The gender of the Sign occupied by the transiting Moon at the moment this aspect forms determines the sex of the child.*

In preparing a fertility cycle, we compute an exact natal horoscope for the woman and note the angle formed between the Sun and Moon. Each month the Sun and the Moon will repeat this same angular relationship. The Signs and Houses play no role in timing the cycle; only the angle is important.

For example, if a woman has the Sun at 5 Pisces 16 and the Moon at 12 Pisces 43, the angular relationship is seven degrees and 27 minutes. In every month, when the Moon is 7°27′ past the Sun, it is the moment of astrological fertility. (The angular relationship is always measured counter-clockwise starting with the New Moon.) *The period of maximum fertility was found to occur twelve to twenty-four hours BEFORE the time the Moon-Sun angle is exact.* In other words, the day preceding the occurrence of the angle is the most fertile day. For contraception, intercourse should be avoided for the three days before each Moon-Sun angle day. The result is 98.2 percent reliable birth control.

The astrological cycle works with the medical cycle. Fifteen days are counted from the *first* day of the last menses to determine the presumed date of ovulation, independent of the regularity and length of the menstrual cycle. When couples use abstinence during the medical as well as astrological fertility cycle doctors report nearly one-hundred percent success in the practice of contraception.

Conversely, intercourse during the medical period, the middle of the menstruation cycle, and during the astrologically fertile period offers the finest assurance of conception. The Sign occupied by the Moon during the astrologically fertile period will determine the sex of the child (Fire and Air Signs, masculine; Water and Earth Signs, feminine).

Computations are not difficult. One notes the lunar aspects to the Sun in a given month, shown in the Ephemeris, and finds the day upon which the Moon is at the same distance (counter-clockwise) from the Sun as it is from the birth Sun in the woman's natal horoscope. The twelve- to twenty-four-hour period of maximum fertility preceding the time of actual Moon-Sun angle allows an approximation exact enough to offer security to a couple. Most often the Moon will not be changing Sign, and gender projection is similarly very easy and secure.

Astrological Predisposition

Research in Astrology has revealed many measurements that suggest a predisposition to fertility or infertility. In planning conception, along with a thorough gynecological examination, these measurements have to be taken into consideration as well.

Astrologer Vivian E. Robson, in his *Astrology and Human Sex Life* (W. Foulsham & Co., Ltd., London; Wehman Bros., Hackensack, N.J., 1963), treats the whole subject of sex, marriage and fertility excellently. He records aphorisms from ancient texts. With regard to a predisposition to "fruitfulness" or "barrenness," the following table is an important guide:

Barren	Semi-barren	Semi-fruitful	Fruitful
Gemini	Aries	Taurus	Cancer
Leo	Sagittarius	Libra	Scorpio
Virgo	Capricorn	Aquarius	Pisces

The relationship between Saturn and the rulers of these Signs, especially in reference to the Vth and VIIth House, is very important. The square, opposition, or conjunction will work against fertility. Neptune in these aspect relationships with the rulers of the Signs will suggest something unknown, some indeterminate factor, some anomaly; perhaps the end result of adoption, when conception is enigmatically impossible.

The woman whose horoscope appears on page 134 had a long history of futility in trying to conceive. She had been tested in every medical way almost constantly throughout the last seven years. Every test had been negative; i.e., there was no medical reason why she could not conceive. Her husband as well was perfectly normal and had had children in a previous marriage. Even artificial insemination was tried, also to no avail. Psychologically, the woman and her husband hoped for children within a very happy and loving marriage. No psychological problems were apparent.

Preparation of her chart for an astrological conception plan revealed many measurements suggesting a predisposition to infertility:

- the Moon in Capricorn, dispositor of the Sun, in XII; Capricorn Ascendant
- the Moon opposed the Sun
- Gemini on the cusp of the Vth
- Mercury, ruler of Gemini, conjunct Venus in Leo, intercepted in VII; opposed Saturn, retrograde within the Ascendant and dispositor of the Moon

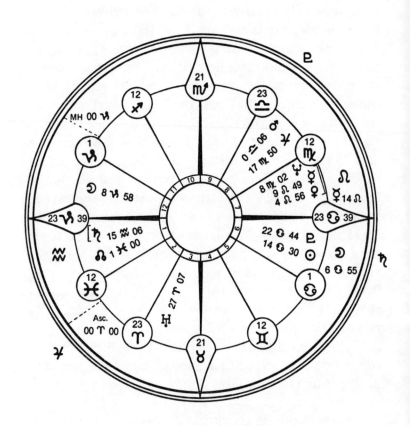

- Moon quincunx Mercury, and Sun quincunx Saturn; Saturn-Mercury opposition axis I-VII, the only emphasis within the chart that is within the Angles
- Moon ruling VI (sickness) and VII (marriage) and in its detriment in XII, ruled by Saturn.

She came for her appointment as the progressed Ascendant exactly opposed her natal Mars; as her progressed Midheaven squared her Mars; as her progressed Moon opposed its natal position; as progressed Mercury separated from conjunction with Venus; and as transiting Saturn conjoined the Sun. The astrological conception plan was made but probably will be unable to overcome the apparent indisposition to fertility.

The horoscope on page 136 is that of a woman with nine children. Although a semi-barren Sign is upon the Vth House and its ruler is in Capricorn, also thought semi-barren, the Ascendant and its ruler are in a fruitful Sign, as is Saturn, trine the Sun and sextile Mars. The Moon is in conjunction with Jupiter, dispositor of the Moon, which is in Scorpio, a fruitful Sign, within the Ascendant.

This woman's husband is also a Scorpio, with the Moon in Scorpio also; Pluto in Cancer.

These ancient assignations are not to be held as absolute. But they do guide the process of deduction. They are of the same nature as the aphorism, "A double-bodied Sign placed upon the VIIth suggests plural marriages": the

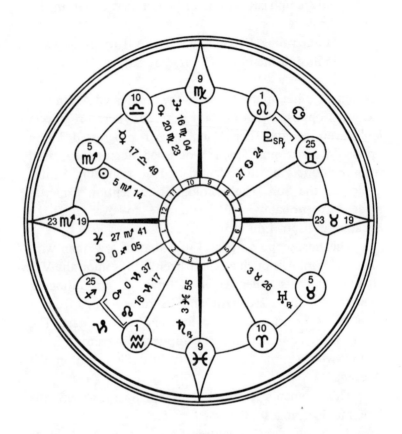

possibility is definite, but synthesis must elaborate and substantiate the deduction.

Conclusion

There are no "magic measurements" for any dimension of life exerience. Although scientific method searches and preaches, the measurement of behavior seen astrologically is dependent upon the interrelation of many parts, if the meaning of the whole is to be grasped, and this whole is dependent upon its relationship with various other environments at different levels. Understanding these complexities demands that we tune in to our instinctive store of behavioral knowledge internalized within our own learning processes. Refining what we understand demands that we learn more, that we seek through deduction to respect the whole identity. Our Astrology is only as evolved as we, the astrologers, are. The magic measurement is the agape, the love for others that we have within.

But there are vast problems to consider in this area as well: the technocracy tends to alienate the individual in his or her wholeness, to isolate efficiency at the expense of expressivity, to extrapolate the part from the whole, to give survival only to the fittest. There is no greater frustration within man than the difficulty in making relationships: with spirit, with goals, with others. The relationship with the astrologer is often a vital, life-changing beginning in the process of relationship. And this relationship must be one of sharing—not moralization, not further alienation, not dogma.

I remember vividly a client who came to me two

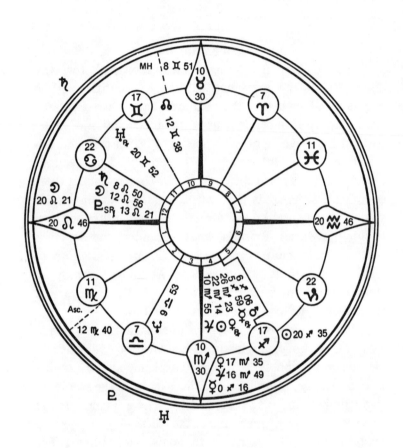

months ago. His horoscope was very difficult (see page 138): the Scorpio group in IV was square the Leo group in XII. The personality image was besieged (Moon within the triple conjunction in XII) but yearning for personal change, rebirth (Leo Moon applying to conjunction with Pluto). Uranus, ruler of VII (relationships) was retrograde in XI (love received) but made no major aspect with any other body in the horoscope. Only a quincunx with the Sun was there, suggesting perhaps a fatalistic dimension to the heavy crosses the man bore, the hurt to pride (Leo).

Emotional and mental frustrations and preoccupations were suggested through Venus and Mercury retrograde. There was no opposition, no focus. What did appear in extremely high focus was a tremendous hurt pride and ego debilitation stemming from the home and the parental influence.

The man was approaching his twenty-eighth birthday. The progressed Sun was exactly trining the Ascendant and opposing Uranus. This was the time when he would somehow successfully project his personality more easily than ever before and break away from the routine loneliness of his past.

What sustained this man was a deep religious sensitivity (Jupiter in Scorpio in conjunction with the Sun and Venus in IV, the soul). This dimension was internalized through the Mercury-Mars conjunction in Jupiter's Sagittarius, Mars ruling the IXth, through Mercury's trine with the Moon, Saturn, and Pluto. Additionally, Neptune supported his religious awareness and the communication of his spirit through its sextiles with Saturn, Mars, Mercury, and the Moon, all in development with the Scorpio Sun (Neptune semi-square the Sun). The matrix of the unconscious (Volume V) was very much a vital dimension of this horoscope (Water Signs, outer planets, Houses IV, VIII, and XII). He was in touch with this store of energy, hopefully harmoniously.

When he arrived, he appeared introverted, subdued, though eager. His talk was open to the extreme. His ability to go deeply into normally inaccessible thoughts and feelings was tremendous. He sensed his life was changing and he sought direction.

One extremely important dimension was clear in his physical presence but not easily deduced through his horoscope: his facial features were strange. His eyes were extremely deeply set (resembling those often seen in a psychic) and his brow and mouth seemed to twist strangely in opposite directions. It was uncomfortable to look at him, though he was not ugly. I felt within me the socially conditioned feelings of avoidance, suspicion of kookiness, something abnormal. But deep discussion revealed a most earnest soul, a bright, spiritual being resigned philosophically to his loneliness and his routine job, and his private joys. I realized how negatively others would instinctively react to him. I saw through testings of his past how he had been rejected time and time again for no reason apparent to him. I felt I knew the answer: that no one had given him acceptance, a chance, an opportunity. No one could get by the externals that too much condition the mechanics of social response within relationships.

Noting the progression of the Sun to trine with the Ascendant and opposition to Uranus, the approach of the progressed Moon to the Ascendant sextile Uranus, the approach of transiting Saturn to its return, Uranus to the fourth cusp, and Pluto to Neptune, I felt secure that this man's spirit and human pride would prevail, would create a new projection for him with less complication than ever before, within the very near future. The most important thing now, at the beginning of this period, would be to have someone believe in him.

Instinctively, I stopped in mid-analysis. I felt love for this man—not compassion. I felt his growth potential and his earnest desire. I had measured his self-awareness and I knew he was strong.

I explained to him that he did not need to have his horoscope done yet; that there was nothing "wrong" any more. I applauded his self-awareness, and I returned to him his payment for the consultation.

He was startled at first, fearful. Then, perceiving my sincerity, he relaxed. We talked about religion, love, the coldness of modern realities . . . through his eyes and mine. And, as we did, his facial features relaxed. He positively radiated comfort. He said, "You're the first person who has never taken advantage of me . . . the first person to really care what I feel." I suggested that that was perhaps why we were together.

We walked to the door together. I put my arms

around him and told him that together we believed in his strengths and that his life would open to him shortly, that God would be helpful. He left in peace and pride. In that time together, perhaps agape and philia had risen to create relationship, to share in service one person's time in its fulness.

3

Illness

Work and love—these are the basics.
Without them there is neurosis.
—*Dr. Theodore Reik*

What causes illness? Why are some people susceptible to certain illnessess and not to others? Why does the occurrence of illness reflect levels of frustration, psychological balance? Does illness *invade* our organic systems? Does a predisposition to it already *pervade* every organism, waiting to be triggered by some unnatural imbalance?

An answer has been known to esotericists and philosophers for ages: illness occurs when the body and spirit are not one. In the psychological age, we may add *mind* to spirit. Astrologically, we can inspect the questions surrounding illness with the premise that *illness reflects an imbalance, a breakup of relationships.*

Illness is caused by a relationship that has become overly tense, imbalanced, frustrated; by a need tension that is unresolved, unfulfilled. Certain people are susceptible to certain kinds of tension, certain kinds of needs that can invite the onset of illness when the frustration of these needs exceeds the tolerances of the organism. The organism becomes predisposed to illness when the balance

143

between its needs and their fulfillment becomes severely upset.

The unresolved need tensions may refer to nutritional needs within the body, to physical relationships with the environment, and to psychological need relationships within opportunities for personal expression and interpersonal cooperation.

Man is susceptible to bacteria and viruses in his relationship with the natural world, to accidents in his relationship with the material environment. Nutritionally, man must respond to the needs within his own organism; psychologically and socially, he must respond to the needs he seeks to fulfill within his relationships. Men and women have strengths and weaknesses that are working continuously to develop under specific need tensions. It is with respect to these psychological, social, and often nutritional concerns that Medical Astrology can be of important service.

The study of sickness is not confined to the VI-XII House axis, the planets present in these Houses, their aspect condition, and that of the rulers of these Houses. Viewed in a psychological frame of reference, Medical Astrology must go beyond this initial topographical focus. It must extend to *any* developmental tension within the horoscope: any planets in square, opposition, and, often, conjunction with each other imply a developmental, behavioral tension within the horoscope, i.e., needs seeking fulfillment through relationships; en route to fulfillment, there will necessarily be varying levels of frustration, reflected in progressions and transits. *Illness can occur in terms suggested by the planets and Houses involved, as life develops in its fulness, as tensions seek resolution, and needs gain fulfillment.*

During analysis of hundreds of horoscopes, I have inspected the health profile of clients by naming every zone of tension within the horoscope, translating the planetary symbolisms into anatomical and pathological references. I was assuming that every developmental tension registered in the horoscope would manifest itself at some time or another (triggered by progressions and transits) in terms of illness.

The results were often correct to the point of being all-inclusive; always, the predominantly most focused of the developmentally tense aspects was precisely correct. The degree of accuracy was supported most reliably when the aspect configurations under analysis did indeed relate to the VI-XII axis, but this was not necessarily always the case. Wherever the aspect configurations related, they were important and of obvious concern in the client's health profile.

The horoscope shown on page 146 indicates several stress points, points of concern for the health profile:

- The Sign on the XIIth, specially important here because the Moon in its detriment is exactly conjunct the cusp and is opposed Uranus in Cancer (the Moon's Sign, the Sign upon the VIth): we could assume that the knees (Capricorn) and stomach (Cancer) would be susceptible to illness in relation to tensions within the self. The stomach

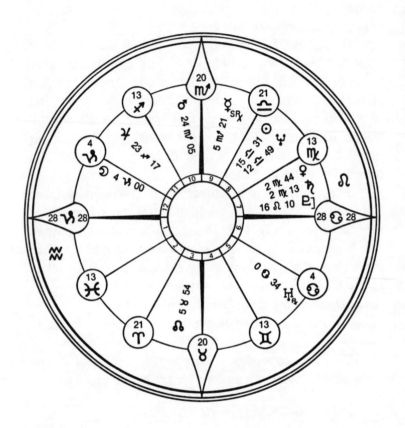

problems would probably be in the form of an ulcer (Uranus, nerves).

- Saturn is dispositor of the Moon and rules the XIIth and the Ascendant. Saturn is conjunct Venus, dispositor of the Sun and Neptune in Libra (characterologically already an indication of emotional tension, constraint, difficulties with relationships). This suggests further illness potentials: the lower back (Libra), the kidneys (Libra, Venus; the blood function symbolized by Neptune). This consideration is very important because the Sun and Neptune are squared by the Moon.

These two configurations cover all the developmentally tense aspects within the horoscope. The native corroborated every deduction right down the line: knees, stomach ulcer, lower back problems, bladder and kidney infections, and added her extreme concern for, yet abuse of her diet (Virgo, Sign of the Saturn and Venus conjunction).

Medical Symbolism

The finest reference book on Medical Astrology extant is the *Encyclopaedia of Medical Astrology*, third revised edition, by Dr. H. L. Cornell (St. Paul, Minnesota: Llewellyn Publications, 1972). Nine-hundred and fifty pages cover the astrological concomitants of diseases of all kinds. The book is indispensible.

Planets

Mercury will always symbolically refer to the nervous system in terms of illness. In aspect configurations with other planets, the dimension of the nerves will be brought into consideration. Mercury in Cancer, for example, will suggest a nervous stomach, if Mercury is within a developmentally tense relationship with another planet; in Aries, headaches from nervous tension; in Virgo, bowel problems; in Taurus, the thyroid or larynx, etc.

Venus under aspect tension suggests illness that comes from *excess* (e.g., gout); illness within the bladder, the kidneys; the hair; the venous blood; often a susceptibility to strep throat (ruler of Taurus); hemorrhoids. Venus (and Jupiter) must be in strong aspect configurations with Mars, Saturn, and/or the trans-Saturnian planets for the specified illness to flourish. (See Hitler's horoscope, page 96).

Mars suggests inflammation, fever, cuts, surgery. As ruler of Aries, the intensity of an important aspect configuration involving Mars may register as migraine headaches, for example, or as an acid stomach when Mars is in Cancer. When Mars is retrograde, the system's ability to deploy energy and will is debilitated and susceptibility to illness is heightened.

Jupiter represents predominantly the liver. Its involvements with Mars, Saturn, Uranus, Neptune, and Pluto are very important measurements of the "expansiveness" of disease, the scope of illness. As the liver assimilates the nourishment within the body (as opportunities order need fulfillment within behavior),

Jupiter is linked with Saturn in the diagnosis of cancer. In almost 100 percent of the many cases studied by Doris Chase Doane and the Church of Light throughout thirty years, cancer patients showed Saturn and Jupiter prominent within the natal horoscope and under heavy stress with the Moon. The progressed charts of these patients showed all of them with progressed aspects to Saturn and Jupiter at the time of cancer development.

Saturn represents colds, constriction, debilitation, and the chronic dimensions of illness. By rulership of Capricorn, it often involves reference to the knees. When placed in Libra, it symbolizes a disfunction of the lower back, the vertebrae at the beltline. Saturn rules depression, melancholy, stoppages, stagnations; a diminution of the minerals of the body; the teeth; the skin. Venus, Jupiter, and Saturn often work together in cases of acne or diabetes: the indulgence in sweets correlated with a Venus supported in a trine or sextile within the horoscope as well as with a Saturn and/or Jupiter under tension elsewhere or with Venus, bringing the tension to the skin's surface and to the insulin supply.

Uranus (with Mercury) refers to the nervous system, usually in the dimension of ego-assertion or intensification of the self. Uranus adds a suddenness to the onset of illness, usually in parallel with the suddenness of frustration experienced in fulfilling the ego's needs. Uranus opens the system to temperamental explosions and self-victimization through accident, usually in relationship with Mars (See Volume VII); the dangers of electricity and shock.

Neptune rules the vagaries, the malaise illnesses, diseases difficult to diagnose. Neptune acts symbolically as a supressor of the self. There is a strong relationship between Neptune and blood disorders. Obsession, disillusionment, loss of mental acuity are all suggested by Neptune in developmentally tense constructs.

Pluto suggests the perspective that either embraces need tensions within reality or projects an unreal perspective that can cause mental imbalance (especially in relationship with Mercury). Such an imbalance of self-perspective is often a concomitant of suicide: the need for death in order to escape the tensions generated by relationships.

Signs

The Signs' rulerships of the body and its organs are as follows (much more detail is available in the Cornell *Encyclopaedia,* of course):

> **Aries:** the head, the region above the brow, the arteries of the head and brain (often affected in correspondence with Jupiter in Aries).
>
> **Taurus:** the throat and its arteries, the larynx, the jugular veins.
>
> **Gemini:** the breath, lungs, the nerve fibers; the shoulders, arms, and hands; the oxygenaticn of the blood.
>
> **Cancer:** the stomach, the breasts, the digestive system.
>
> **Leo:** the heart, life itself, the back.
>
> **Virgo:** the lower abdomen, the intestines, the bowels; hygiene, diet.

Libra: the kidneys, the lower back, the fallopian tubes, the distillation of urine; the veins.

Scorpio: the reproductive organs in the male and the female; the rectum and the colon; the clitoris; menstruation.

Sagittarius: the hips, thighs, and the sciatic nerve.

Capricorn: knees, joints, bones (with Saturn); dryness and infertility.

Aquarius: the calves and ankles, the saphenous vein.

Pisces: the feet; the lymphatic system; phlegm, mucus.

Reflex Action and Sympathy

Throughout medical analysis of the horoscope, the Sun and Moon relationship is paramount. The lights represent the polarity of life's essence, the characterological thrust in toto of the entire organism. Any developmental tension between them will be reflected through the parents in early life, through significances carried through into maturation, into developmental relationships with all things. The lights illuminate life-energy. Specifically, the Sun rules the heart and spine; the Moon rules the stomach and the emotions; the Sun rules the right eye of the male and the left eye of the female; the Moon rules the right eye of the female and the left eye of the male.

With such emphasis on the importance of relationship, the reciprocity and reflection between need and fulfillment, between cause and effect, there is a relationship internally within astrological indices of illness: *the Sign opposite the Sign involved within a developmental tension must also be considered in diagnosis.* This phenomenon within synthesis is called "reflex action" or "sympathy." For example: among the Cardinal Signs, Aries opposes Libra. A tension relating to Aries-concerns in illness will often have a reflex action, a sympathy response within Libra illness-concerns: headaches and fever are often vitally important symptoms of kidney problems as well as nerve inflammation along the spine; Cancer opposes Capricorn, and the zones of these two Signs will often be in sympathy to one another. In fact, the four Cardinal Signs, forming a Grand Cross, will have to be considered in response to a developmental tension within *any* one or two of the Cardinal Signs.

The same applies to the Fixed Cross and the Mutable Cross, the sympathetic units formed by the four Signs in the other two modalities. For example, the removal of part of the sex organs (Scorpio) will affect the voice (Taurus); heart trouble (Leo) will often cause swelling of the ankles (Aquarius); upper respiratory ailments (Gemini) are often said to be caused by having wet feet (Pisces); bad diet (Virgo) invites liver problems (Sagittarius, Jupiter); weak knees (Capricorn), weak stomach (Cancer) and spinelessness (Libra) are all interchangeable, suggesting insecurity or anxiety.

Health and Vitality

There is a difference between health and vitality: one can be vital in energy, robust in recuperative power, but of bad health; or healthy and not at all vital. *Any* aspect between Mars and the lights will give vitality; the conditions of the whole synthesis will suggest the health profile. Illness seen within a vital system will be more easily overcome by intrinsic recuperative powers (Mars and the lights).

The horoscope example on page 154 shows a woman with an intense ego drive (Sun in Aries), preoccupied with establishing a strong identity perspective (square Pluto) in her home (Pluto in IV), through her marriage and all her relationships (Pluto rules Scorpio intercepted in VII). She has a difficult time doing this (Sun in XII) and certainly doesn't enjoy her husband's enthusiasm (Jupiter retrograde in VII), though he is probably very tolerant (Jupiter trine with Pluto; Venus, ruler of VII, sextile Pluto). Her energy for ego presentation "goes in before it goes out" (Mars retrograde). The nervous tension builds up tremendously (Mercury in XII opposed Mars, dispositor of the Sun and placed in VI). The potentials for idealistic self-deception within this whole scheme of things (Moon conjunct Neptune in Virgo in VI) certainly do not help matters. The body is prone to react to frustrations in the form of illnesses whenever her needs and energies are frustrated.

Based upon this abbreviated capsule-sketch of the horoscope, let us inspect what the illness responses could be:

- Saturn is ruler of the Midheaven and is upon the twelfth cusp in opposition with Neptune and the Moon, semi-square the Sun; Mercury rules Virgo on VI, is the dispositor of Moon-Neptune, is opposed Mars retrograde in VI, and is in Aries in XII.

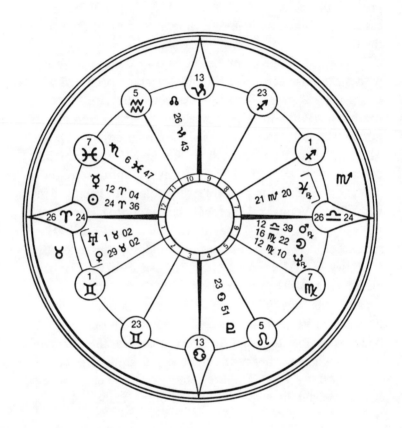

Additionally, Mercury semi-squares Venus, dispositor of Mars, ruler of the Ascendant: her high nervous reactions about her ego thrust and its frustrations will manifest themselves through her skin (Saturn), probably in the form of rashes, inflammations, hives (Mars), upsetting her self-esteem in terms of personal appearance and beauty (Mars, ruler of Ascendant, retrograde in Libra; Venus semi-square Mercury). This condition will probably be complicated by a bad diet (Virgo) and bad nutrition.

In this example, there is a reflex reaction between Moon-Neptune in Virgo and Saturn in Pisces because of the opposition. We can expect a sympathy between Gemini (ruled by Mercury) and Sagittarius as well (Jupiter retrograde): under pressure the woman is highly susceptible to common colds and possibly liver complications from her diet deficiencies.

Through the opposition Aries-Libra, the reflex reactions are automatically noted. The sympathy with the other two Cardinal Signs is also already included in the diagnosis through Saturn, ruler of Capricorn, and the Moon, ruler of Cancer.

• Additionally, Mars' disposition of and opposition to Mercury, within an elevated nervous system, and its rulership of the Ascendant and disposition of the Sun—these factors, within the characterological system and the behavior we can anticipate, will suggest strongly the occurrence of migraine

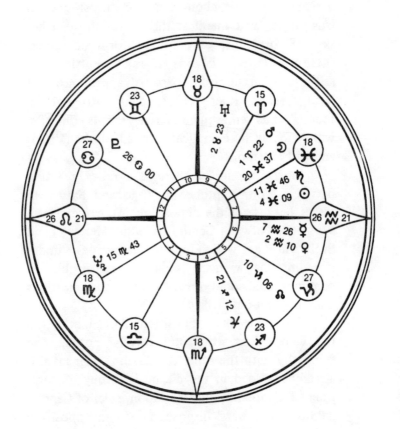

headaches (Aries) under tension; pains in the lumbar region (Libra), affecting the sciatic nerve down the sides of the legs (Sagittarius); kidney infections (Libra, Mars); high blood pressure (Mars; Neptune); and uncomfortable swelling of the feet (Pisces).

The diagnosis of this profile of illness was made in about thirty seconds during the astrological interview. The native corroborated every deduction precisely.

The second example, on page 156, is extremely simple: the very strong conjunction of the Sun, Saturn, and the Moon, opposed Neptune, with the Moon ruling Cancer on XII and Saturn ruling Capricorn on VI, with Neptune dispositor of the three bodies, and the Sun ruling the Ascendant—these factors suggest eye problems, a weak stomach as well as problems with her feet. The woman has extremely bad eyesight, a very sensitive stomach, and flat feet. These conditions are augmented by the square made by Jupiter to the opposition axis.

Additionally, the horoscope shows Venus and Mercury in VI square Uranus in IX: the woman had an extreme susceptibility to strep throat (Taurus) for the first thirty years of her life, and then began to suffer from frequent bladder infections and gynecological symptoms (reflex action; Venus). She worries much about her hair (Venus) and has colored it blond (Leo Ascendant). She has extremely weak ankles which keep her from ice-skating, something she has always wanted to do. In tension periods in her life, all of these concerns erupt along with an

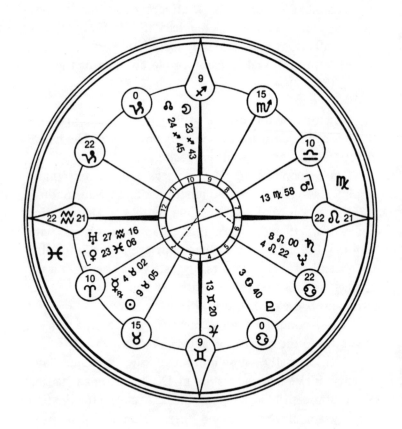

eczema outbreak (Saturn) upon her shoulders (Gemini, sympathetic responses among the Mutable Signs).

In the example on page 158, a heart condition and the time of heart attack were deduced and measured within just a minute or two: Saturn and Neptune are in conjunction in the Sun's Sign, Leo, in the VIth House, ruled by the Moon within a Grand Cross, opposed Jupiter and square Venus and Mars. The Sun and Mercury are square Saturn and Neptune. When transiting Saturn would conjoin the Sun at about age fifty-one to fifty-two, making the (second) closing square to its birth position, the native would be vulnerable to a heart attack, probably from overwork (VIth House emphasis, Moon in X, Mercury oriental and retrograde, Mars in Virgo in VII). The ephemeris showed that this Saturn-Sun conjunction transit occurred in April, 1970, the native's fifty-second birthday month. The ephemeris showed the progressed Sun at fifty-one to fifty-two to be exactly trine Uranus: the native would have extremely fine rallying forces to recover, echoing the vitality dimension of the Mars square with the Moon and trine with the Sun. The native had suffered a heart attack in April, 1970 (two years before astrological consultation), was hospitalized under emergency conditions, and recovered more quickly than could ever have been medically expected.

The example on page 160 shows a woman who has had a very difficult life. Accumulated tensions have been surmounted and, in her late forties and early fifties, she faces well-earned success, a whole new life, with the progressed Sun trining Uranus and crossing the fourth

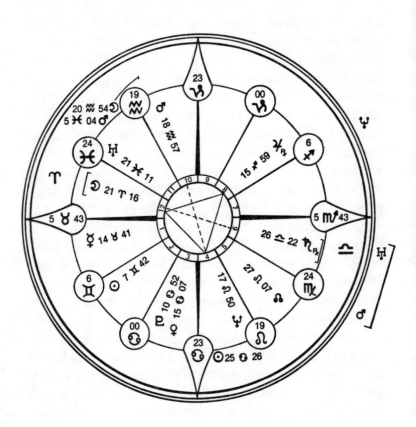

cusp. But the lifework, through much developmental tension, would have accumulated and still threaten the system. The analysis was done by mail in January, 1974 (I have never met the woman). Following the key opposition between the Moon and Saturn retrograde within the XII-VI axis, the Moon within the Fire Grand Trine; with Mars as dispositor of the Moon and opposing Neptune, ruler of XII; with Venus, dispositor of Saturn, square the Moon and conjunct Pluto, I wrote the following caution to her:

> During the period February-October, 1974, your health is in serious condition (*progressed Sun square Saturn; progressed Moon opposed Neptune and conjunct Mars; transiting Neptune opposed Sun, transiting Uranus conjunct Saturn; Mars transiting square the Sun in August and conjunct Saturn in October, 1974*): your spine, nervous system, perhaps your kidneys, blood pressure, and reproductive organs. Extreme care should be exerted; surgical remediation of some kind can be expected [*progressed Mars was applying to a square with the natal Sun*].

After mailing the full analysis of the whole life up to the present and into the next few years, I telephoned her to further explain these health concerns and the threat of illness. We talked in great detail about symptoms, proper medical care and what kind of doctor to go to. Now, in early October, I have just received a telephone call from

Howard Hughes

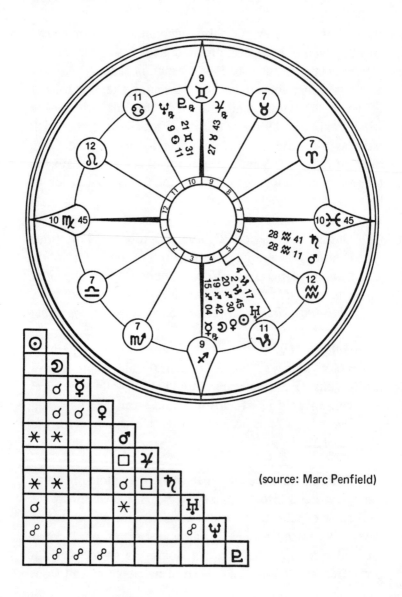

(source: Marc Penfield)

her. Full of gratitude, she assures me that she is in good health, thanks to her observance of the astrological analysis. Everything in her horoscope was true. After having received my caution, she immediately put herself in the care of a competent physician who right away diagnosed and successfully treated several conditions suggested by her horoscope. "Isn't it wonderful, Mr. Tyl, that I received your letter in time. Your warning may have saved my life."

Hypochondria

The relationship between the mind and body is dramatically established when psychological fears or tensions become so great that they *create* real or imagined physical sicknesses. Hypochondria is an escape or defense mechanism. Freud called it "flight into illness": the ego feels it gains the advantage of escaping fears or tensions by becoming sick. Relationship is disrupted to gain attention or avoid the threat of frustration. As suggested in Volume V, page 123, this condition can be seen within a horoscope in fear significators (strong aspects to the Sun, Moon, especially involving Saturn and Neptune) relating to the VI-XII axis and its rulers.

The horoscope of Howard Hughes, on page 162, shows this vividly. This hypochondriacal billionaire recluse has Mercury, Moon, Venus, and the Sun opposed Pluto at the Midheaven; the Sun is conjunct Uranus; Uranus and the Sun rule the VI-XII axis and oppose Neptune. Uranus is dispositor of Mars and Saturn in strong conjunction in VI, both square Jupiter in Taurus, ruled by Venus. The rulers of his Midheaven, Ascendant, VIth and XIIth Houses, the dispositors of every body within the horoscope are all involved within "affliction" configurations; they are also under tension. Like Mercury, ruler of the Midheaven and Ascendant, all the planets above the horizon are retrograde. There is no trine within the horoscope. The sextiles support the flight into illness. The IVth House symbolically becomes the XIIth!

How difficult these tensions are. The enormously powerful axis that dominates the horoscope is the IV-X, parental, professional axis. A powerful administrative perspective is established. Because of insecurities inherited from his parents, Hughes fears his own power and drive. His motives are not clear even to himself. Perhaps he senses with almost debilitating sensitivity his potential for erratic behavior (Mars-Saturn in VI), the risk he runs with bad judgments in response to his soaring imagination (Sun-Neptune) and intense nervous creativity (Sun-Uranus and Neptune). His show to the public cannot be allowed to fail. He needs to be shielded. Perhaps he fears letting down his father's expectations of him. We can conjecture that fear of sexual inadequacy haunts him as well (Saturn rules V, is dispositor of Sun and Uranus). The whole complex fights internally with his need to be identified personally with all he does (Venus oriental). The whole complex of hypochondriacal flight is rationalized by his feeling of comfort and efficiency in working within the home (Moon in IV).

Hypochondria exists in every person to one degree or another. It is a very accessible escape-defense mechanism.

It is an important clue to times of tension, when needs are pressing for fulfillment and the system senses how important fulfillment is. Awareness of this phenomenon gives depth to the understanding of Saturn's symbolism: it is ambition and its needs; it is also constriction, melancholy, and reclusiveness.

Nutrition

With the passage of Pluto through Cancer in 1913 through 1939, the perspectives of world security were jolted by two world wars. In matters of health, the major concerns were getting enough to eat during a time of depression and general scarcity. The reflex action of Capricorn was always in evidence. Stomach ailments were "in fashion."

As Pluto transited Leo in 1939 through 1957, medical perspectives were changed by the therapeutic development of X-rays, ultrasonics, and atomic science (reflex from Aquarius) to a very high level. Heart research became intensified. Heart disease became recognized as the major "natural" killer.

Pluto transited Virgo in 1957 through 1972 when nervous ailments, nervous "breakdowns," became the popular illnesses. Calming down (Pisces) became the catch-all counsel for neurotic symptoms and anxieties. Dietary and nutritional studies flooded the market as never before. The natural food movement was born. With Pluto's entrance into Libra in 1972, the spine gained prominence; bad backs are replacing nervous disorders as the primary socio-medical complaint (in direct relationship to the

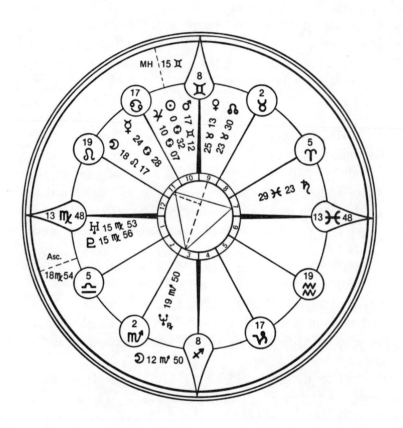

increase of leisure time and diminution of exercise and physical labor). The Aries reflex is seen in the current intense study of brain-wave control to help the individual find fulfillment and to improve his outlook.

Stomach concerns, "filling the bread-basket," heart disease, nutrition, nervous anxiety, bad backs are all still with us. Awareness of cancer has been intensified during the past decade, and there is conjecture that it is viral in origin (Virgo). Social unrest (Libra) now tends to upset the spine of society. Concern with nutrition is perhaps all-pervasive within these areas of highly focused medical research. "You are what you eat" has arched its significance over Pluto's transit of one quarter of the Zodiac, from Cancer to Libra within the last six decades.

The nutritional needs of the human organism are ruled by the Moon astrologically. The Sign Cancer is also extremely important, based upon the nurturing symbolisms of motherhood and the breast. Venus, especially during childhood, is important as a measurement of nutrition assimilated for growth with special attention to the kidneys (eliminating wastes and body poisons). After adolescence, Uranus rules the main significance of individual growth.

The horoscope shown on page 166 is that of a young German girl whose parents came to me in great anxiety when she was nearing her seventh birthday. Helga had developed a dry, nervous cough that hacked about every thirty seconds constantly throughout the day, except when she was preoccupied. She also had a nervous twitching of the eyes and a sharp twist of the head that seemed to follow the cough immediately every time.

She was in her first year of school, seldom spoke, yet she showed precocious artistic talent and seemed to be quite content with her world as it was. She had an older sister who did brilliantly in school, appeared over-disciplined, cool, aloof, almost too perfect to be believed in all her behavior. The parents were in their late forties, rigid though not austere, and constantly concerned about their children. The husband was a very successful businessman (his horoscope appears in Volume VI, page 152).

The parents wanted to take drastic action. They planned to take Helga to a neurosurgeon for extensive testing. The child had already been overtested for reading disability and speech problems; had been placed in all sorts of classes to learn swimming, painting and music. The child seemed beseiged by parental concern for her precocious bloom. The parents wanted to know, as "the next to last resort," if Astrology could help them.

The horoscope shows a very powerful little girl: Uranus and Pluto are in exact conjunction within the Ascendant, square Mars in the Midheaven (the nervous cough: Mars in Gemini). The Moon is in Leo and is dispositor of the Sun and Jupiter in X. Mercury rules the Ascendant and the Midheaven, is the dispositor of Uranus, Pluto, and Mars, and is within a Water Grand Trine (not involving the Sun or Moon) with Saturn and Neptune. Her potential for intense personal projection, her self-awareness perspective (Uranus-Pluto) was highly charged with developmental tension (square with Mars). This tension was diffused throughout her personality and supported her needs well through the Mars sextile with the Moon in Leo. She would project these theatrical ego needs to gain love and appreciation (Moon rules Cancer on XI). Yet, there would be an emotional detachment (Grand Trine in Water without the Sun or Moon) and an emotional self-sufficiency that could develop. She would be inscrutable (Neptune), perhaps appearing inaccessible, constrained, cold (Saturn), yet always aware of her needs for security and love, for having these communicated to her (Mercury in Cancer in XI). Helga constantly played tricks on her parents, pretending to fall, to be in trouble, to have been hurt, in order to have her over-reacting parents come running to her. The sobs would immediately turn into a private smile of triumph.

Her best line of communication of herself was definitely through art (all corroborated by her fascinating paintings since age 4). Venus opposes Neptune in the Grand Trine, the access to and exit from the Grand Trine. Her mother was intensely involved with the promotion of this channel of Helga's expression (Venus conjunct the nodal axis).

The introversion, repression of self within relationships, is seen through the Sun-Saturn square. Within all of this, the nervous system is extremely high-strung (Mars square to Uranus and Pluto in the Ascendant; Mercury ruling Ascendant and Midheaven). The time in her seventh year was critical through progression of the Midheaven to exact square with Uranus-Pluto. The problem required thorough analysis of the family's interaction with Helga, to understand her very complicated personality. But, en route to that goal, perhaps nutritional support could relieve the nervous behavioral symptoms (the child was frail, weak-looking): the Moon squared the Venus-Neptune axis, the outlet and inroad to the Grand Trine.

At the time of this consultation, I was working with a homeopathic specialist in Germany, both of us trying to learn more about the relationships between the planetary symbolisms and aspect relationships and the laws of nutrition. Research also included many of the nutrition books popular today, and special attention was given to medical-nutritional symbolism offered in Dr. Cornell's encyclopedia and other volumes.

The Moon configuration focused nutritional analysis upon magnesium phosphate, ruled by the Sign Leo, the salt that supplies the nerve sheaths; potassium ruled by Neptune; potassium chloride ruled by Gemini; and the system's difficulty in extracting vitamins from food, revealed by Saturn square or opposed Mars (or Saturn retrograde in Cancer). The square aspect was developing in Helga's horoscope.

In a report to the family, the specialist and I concluded, in part, as follows:

- Biochemically, an inspection of the horoscope in great detail suggests that the energy taken into the body through food is not being well-assimilated by the system. There appears to be a deficiency in magnesium and Vitamin B-6.

- Helga's probable deficiency in magnesium causes her to become irritable, high-strung, sensitive to noise, hyperexcitable, apprehensive, and possibly belligerent. Such a deficiency is difficult for a physician to detect because it remains largely inside the cells of the body; the quantity in the blood plasma varies very little. Such deficiencies occur commonly where foods are eaten that have been grown in chemically fertilized fields.

- Magnesium is needed by every cell in the body, including those in the brain. It is essential for the synthesis of proteins, for the utilization of fats and carbohydrates, and for hundreds of enzyme systems, especially those involved in energy production. Magnesium is a natural tranquilizer.

- In children, the balance between magnesium and calcium is very important. The proportion should be two parts of calcium to one part of magnesium. For Helga, amplifying her diet with a magnesium compound to the amount of 500 mgs may conspicuously help her nervous system and the assimilation of food-energy. Magnesium compound powder (not magnesium oxide) can be bought in any drugstore; 500 mgs, ½ teaspoonful, added to juice or milk once a day.

- Vitamin B-6 as well should be supplemented: 25-50 mgs twice a day to begin, then once a day. This vitamin is essential for the acids from protein to be utilized by the body. Together, magnesium and vitamin B-6 added to the diet daily will make energy assimilation in the body more efficient; nervousness will be reduced, and the organism will have more energy to express itself.

The father took this part of the report to his family doctor, who concurred with it totally. Some other supplements were added (potassium), and the nutritional remedy was begun immediately. In two days, the cough and facial tic were almost entirely gone!

The parents were thrilled, and all their energy was channeled into deeper work within the family situation to help make the environment and relationships more comfortable for Helga. The young girl had a very deep feeling of being lost in the shadow of her sister (Pluto rules III, sisters, and is conjunct Uranus, individuality, in the Ascendant; Neptune in III squared the Moon). Although she could not communicate emotions easily, she interpreted all situations in an emotional way (Grand Trine). Proximity, peace and quiet, touching were all very important to her. She would rebel against organization or formalized attention, when her own will and level of sensitivity were not respected. Parental protection would take away her stage-opportunities (Moon in Leo), and Helga needed to play out her own drama her own way. Her greatest need was freedom *to initiate expression,* to win individual ascendance in relation to her sister. With new energy, less structure, more self-pride and improved health, her tensions would flow more successfully, aiding her development.

The nutritional analysis and more details not included here were worked out carefully and thoroughly checked with a medical specialist. The deductions were made astrologically, supported by a medical specialist, and they served a child and her family superbly. The case is not finished, however, because the problems will take on other levels of frustration as the progressed Moon opposes Mars and squares Uranus-Pluto in the spring of 1976. At that time, however, the progressed Sun will conjoin Jupiter, suggesting excellent rallying forces through a parent (Jupiter rules IV). The most positive time for full maturation may be the progressed Sun's trine to Saturn at age twenty-nine, with Saturn's transit return.

Astrologers can gain great facility with nutritional analysis through further study of diet and translation of what is learned into astrological deductions. To begin with, these keys will be helpful: the Sun rules the vitamins; the Moon rules the nourishment stability within the body; Mercury rules the air, the smoke, the pollution we breathe; Venus rules carbohydrates; Mars rules proteins; Jupiter rules fats; and Saturn rules the stabilizing salts.

Elbert Benjamine, in his excellent book *Stellar Dietetics* (Chicago: Aries Press, 1942; out of print), studies the relationship between nutrition and Astrology in great detail. Translation of bodily function into Astrology proceeds this way: physical and electromagnetic energy comes from the relationship-union of oxygen (Mercury) with food taken into the body. Excess of food beyond the oxygen supply leads to lethargy, sluggishness. Deep breathing relieves the situation, disposes of the product of combustion and affords oxygen for further combustion. Fatigue is dissipated and energy is supplied. The energy that is generated in this fuel combustion process is what we call calories. Benjamine's style of thinking is a model for all of us to follow in further studies (pp. 15-16):

> People with a prominent Venus crave sweets. But they may not be able to completely digest cane sugar and some forms of starch if Venus is also afflicted. Furthermore, if Jupiter is prominent and afflicted, too much of the sweets, and particularly those made from cane sugar, may lead to impure blood stream and blemishes, such as pimples, which mar the complexion, or to the development of diabetes. This because of inadequate insulin supply to handle the great demands made upon it.

Throughout his book, he offers dietary suggestions to offset the symbolism of planets under tension ("affliction"). These thoughts have been brought up to date by Doris Chase Doane in her excellent book, *Astrology: 30 years Research* (Los Angeles, California, 1956). On page 131, she writes:

- With the Sun afflicted, the physical diet needs iodine, manganese, vitamin B complex and vitamin A. *The mental diet* needs harmonious thoughts of vitality and power. (Benjamine and Doane's work within the Church of Light research stressed the power of the thought processes to correct deficiencies within the system. Thoughts are "magnetic," inviting psychological dispositions to help or hinder the unity and health of identity.)

- With the Moon afflicted, a proper water-salt balance and vitamin B-2 are needed; and harmonious Mars thoughts of the aggressive type.
- Mercury afflicted: calcium, vitamin B-1, vitamin D or sunlight; harmonious Jupiter thoughts of the religious or philosophical kind.
- Venus afflicted: iodine, copper, vitamin A and E; harmonious Sun (vitality and power) and Saturn thoughts (safety and care).
- Mars afflicted: iron, low protein (but a variety), vitamins A, B-1, and C; harmonious Moon thoughts (domesticity, security).
- Jupiter afflicted: sulfur, care with sugar and fat; harmonious Mercury thoughts (intellectual).
- Saturn afflicted: variety in mineral salts, vitamins, proteins, harmonious Venus (social) and Sun thoughts (vitality, power).
- Uranus afflicted: calcium, vitamin B-1, vitamin D or sunlight; harmonious Saturn (safety and care) and Sun thoughts (vitality and power).
- Neptune afflicted: energy food, calcium, less protein, vitamins D and B-1; harmonious Saturn (safety, care) and Sun thoughts (vitality, power).
- Pluto in affliction configurations: protein, iron, calcium, vitamins A, C, D, B complex; harmonious Mars thoughts (aggression).

This research is invaluable. The relationship is always preserved between the body and the mind, the nutritional needs and their nourishment, tension and fulfillment and between causes of illness and its treatment. Astrologers should study this information in great detail and relate it to the ever-improving nutritional knowledge being published to guide public health. Working carefully with a doctor, a nutritionist, or a dietician will increase the understanding of nutritional analysis within astrological analysis.

Death

Relationship is as important in understanding the concept of death as it is in understanding illness. Ultimately, the self longs for death in order to be *totally rid* of developmental tensions within the process of becoming. This phenomenon is Freud's death-wish, and it is the major psychoanalytic component of suicide.

Many older textbooks in Astrology search for the significators of life and death. There is the measurement of the *hyleg,* the hylegiacal places: parts of the horoscope that are reputed to give greater vitality and endurance to the native when the Sun, Moon, Ascendant, Venus, and/or Jupiter are found there (becoming the Apheta, the "Giver or Preserver of Life"). These places are located as follows: from twenty-five degrees below the Ascendant to five degrees above the Ascendant; from five degrees below the cusp of the IXth House to the middle of the XIth House; from five degrees below the cusp of the VIIth House to twenty-five degrees above this seventh cusp.

The reasoning behind the hylegiacal zones is to give life-saving strengths through the lights and benefics to the

Angles at and above the horizon. No place below the horizon could be thought to have this property.

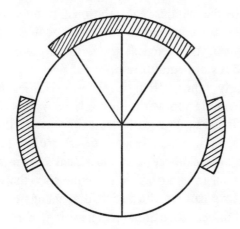

In relationship with the hyleg-apheta concept, there is the questionable concept of the *anareta,* the planet that might destroy life. According to legend and very old texts, any of the planets can act as the anareta, becoming so through severe afflictions to or from planets within the hylegiacal zones at birth, debilitating their life-preserving symbolism.

Through research and discussion with expert astrologers, three major points about the matter of life and death must be made emphatically: the idea of the hyleg is reasonable; the concept of the anareta is *not* reasonable, nor is it reliable to any degree in horoscopes analyzed for death; and, third, death is *not* a matter within the astrologer's scope of service. This discussion is necessary to help mitigate the death mystique that troubles all students, practitioners, and clients, to put the ominous consideration of the anareta far into the background.

Within the premise of relationship tensions, death must be seen as an acute demand upon the *whole* system, a demand tension that exceeds the whole system's potential to rally and restore equilibrium.

Similarly, the VIIIth and IVth Houses have too onerous a reputation within superficial symbolism. The VIIIth House has a link with death because of the natural placement upon this House of Scorpio. *In deeper symbolism,* we can see the individual's own self-value usurped, taken in and over by someone else (the second of the VIIth); we can see the occult dimensions deep within the self plumbed to gain a regenerating, a rejuvenating awareness within the life, such awareness of life almost always being established by an understanding and awareness of death; we can see "inheritances" of many kinds.

The IVth House is usually referred to as symbolizing "death as finalization," perhaps to separate it from the regenerative dimension of the VIIIth House symbolism. We have seen often in analyses throughout this series that the IVth also suggests a new beginning, i.e., one matter ending before another begins.

Indeed, in horoscopes analyzed for death, the VIIIth and IVth Houses gain importance. But analysis of death astrologically can have validity only *after the fact,* and perhaps then the search is useless in terms of astrological service. Instead of succumbing to the fears implicit in the death mystique, we should analyze *for life* in terms of growth within relationships, motivated by tensions to be; in the same way we should absorb and welcome tensions that take away one matter to allow another to grow. In this way, we are placing emphasis upon the hyleg symbolism: the accentuation of self (Ascendant) and others in relationship (Descendant) in order to achieve a zenith of accomplishment through the life experience (Midheaven).

The horoscope example on page 180 shows a woman who, two days after giving birth to a child just before her eighteenth birthday, was pronounced "medically dead." Her system rallied; she came back to life; and now, in her fifties, is a vibrant astrologer, teacher and counsellor. At the time of her hospitalization to have a child, her progressions and transits suggested severe demands upon her system: the progressed Sun was squaring Uranus, the progressed Ascendant was conjunct radical Neptune, which was square the Sun at birth, and the progressed Midheaven opposed Saturn (Saturn rules VI, Neptune rules VIII). Transiting Mars on the crucial day was square the Moon in VIII (Moon rules XII); transiting Pluto (ruler of IV) was conjunct the Ascendant and was square Mars in IV; transiting Jupiter, dispositor of the Sun and ruler of V (children), was square Saturn in IV.

The horoscope indicated extreme duress. Within the debilitation of childbirth, the body in its momentary weakness would have to fight for its life. The Ascendant is extremely important in this example: natal Mars squares

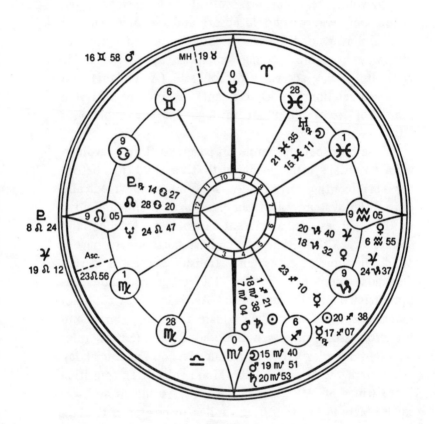

the Ascendant that is ruled by the Sun, and the Sun is square Neptune; the progressed Ascendant is conjunct this Neptune; transiting Pluto is crossing the Ascendant; and the eclipse preceding this date of trauma was an annular eclipse of the Sun on 1 August 1943 at 8 Leo 02, *conjunct the Ascendant and square Mars.* Pluto's transit of this eclipse point would set off the stress symbolism of all the configurations.

The whole period during the last months of this woman's pregnancy was under stress. At one level, the symbolism resting so heavily upon the IVth House could suggest that one life would end (the mother's death) for another life to begin (the birth of the baby). The trauma was caused by the use of some unsterilized instruments (Mars in transit) that affected the woman's whole chemical system (Moon in Pisces) and caused a severe blood infection (natal Neptune-Sun square; Sun sesqui-quadrate, 135° aspect, with Pluto in XII).

The woman's rallying forces—her vitality—are natally strong: Mars trines the Moon and squares the Ascendant; the Sun rules the Ascendant and is in the angular IVth, trine Uranus; there are Fixed Signs on all the Angles; Venus and Jupiter are in conjunction in the VIth, sextile Saturn; there is a Water Grand Trine that gains outlet from Pluto to Venus—Jupiter in VI.

In discussing death, we must always consider the will to live. This will to live has performed miracles within critical trauma. It is the "Mars thought pattern" referred to by Elbert Benjamine and Doris Chase Doane in the Church of Light research. The Mars pattern, the will to live, is *aggression*. It must be repeated that any aspect between Mars and the Sun, Moon, and/or rulers of hylegiacal Angles corresponds to vitality, to rallying forces, to the will to live. Indeed, a tense relationship with Mars may correspond to difficulty but, at the same time, the energy dimensions *deployed by the will* correspond to the saving strength, the extricating quantum.

The planet Pluto has a legendary affinity with death. Pluto was the god of the underworld. Homer described him thus: "Pluto, the grisly god, who never spares, who feels no mercy, who hears no prayers." In the study of Astrology throughout the volumes of this series, Pluto is symbolically framed as the planet of "perspective": the onerous shadow is taken away, the will is respected, the parameters of development are expanded to fit modern times of discovery, opportunity, and grand change. Change of perspective assumes a kind of death; the Phoenix rises only from ashes.

In Volume III, we studied the aspects through short, carefully constructed energy-images. The relationships between Mars and Pluto are particularly revealing: upon Pluto's discovery, within the nineteenth degree of Cancer, Mars was in opposition in the eighteenth degree of Capricorn. Will was in awareness aspect with the symbol of perspective. The world since that time early in 1930 has become truly global through will, through aggression. In an individual's horoscope, Mars opposed Pluto suggests energies, will, that have difficulty tuning in with proper application. The square suggests will and perspective in high developmental tension: escapism, rebellious breakaway from social norms. The conjunction focuses will and perspective intensely, corresponding to subtle controls, underwordly application of the will, detection of perspectives.

Pluto's developmental relationship with any planet in natal aspect, progression, or transit corresponds with an alteration of perspective within that planet's symbolism. Particularly in relationship with Mercury, alteration of perspective often includes a consideration of death, of suicide.

Suicide usually emerges from unrealistic perceptions of the self's position, a loss of defense mechanisms and the inward turning of the death wish finally to rid the self of tension. When Mercury is square Pluto, and Neptune is also prominent, the thoughts of suicide are usually strong in the personality; also, when a debilitated Mars and a planet in House XII—or its ruler—are afflicted, under stress. Additionally, a heavy melancholy is usually involved, a pervasive sadness, reflected in the Sun, Moon, and/or Mercury strongly aspected by Saturn; with Houses VIII and XII emphasized. According to Freud, melancholy involves a withdrawal of creative aggression (libido; Mars) from an object, from living. The ego is then treated as the abandoned object, suffers internalized aggression, and abandons life.

The horoscope example on page 184 shows a suicide attempt when transiting Saturn opposed the natal Moon and Mercury at the same time that transiting Neptune crossed the Ascendant. In the natal configuration, Mercury and the Moon are square Neptune, and Saturn retrograde

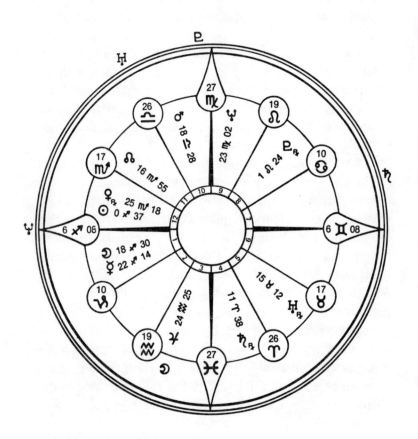

opposes Mars. The Moon and Mercury are in Sagittarius, Sign of the higher mind natural to the IXth House; Neptune, square the Moon and Mercury, is in the IXth in Mercury's Sign. This configuration would suggest a fantasy development within the mind that would affect the personal development in important ways. The only other angular configuration is the Mars-Saturn opposition: will-energy and caution at odds, complicated by a legacy of inferiority feelings (Saturn retrograde) absorbed from the parents (X-IV).

The Sun is in XII, semi-square Mars. The Sun is trine Pluto, ruler of XII. The Houses IV, VIII, and XII are in Water Signs, accented by retrogradation, and the rulers of these Signs (matrix of the unconscious, Volume V) are within key configurations that have the Neptune Midheaven position and square with the rising Moon-Mercury conjunction as the most important point. Finally, Jupiter, ruler of the Ascendant and dispositor of the Moon and Mercury is semi-square Saturn and square Venus retrograde in XII.

The woman is easily depressed, demoralized by unfulfillment and feelings of inferiority. She takes refuge in a do-your-own-thing fantasy existence (Moon in I). Her will is undermined, her ego-protection is emphasized.

As her progressed Moon was in the mental and reactant IIIrd, it squared its own position in the natal configuration, squared Mercury and opposed Neptune. At the same time, transiting Saturn opposed Moon-Mercury from the VIIth. Transiting Pluto had just crossed the Midheaven, and Neptune was exactly upon the Ascendant.

Richard M. Nixon

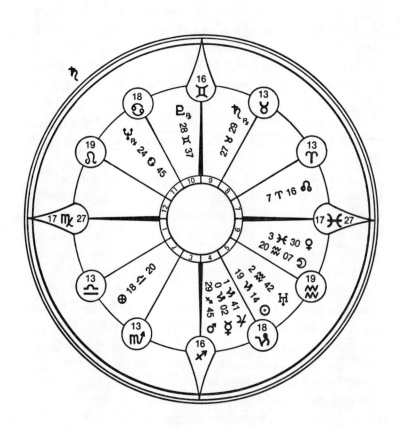

The woman made a suicide attempt, using morphine (Neptune).

Again, there are no magic measurements for suicide, although there are keys. Just as we learn within the socializing process to anticipate certain behavior from certain external and internal symptoms, we learn astrologically to anticipate certain behavior from predispositions, need tensions, and time pressures from certain symbolic keys. What is most telling within this horoscope is that Mercury within the Moon conjunction in the Ascendant and the square with Neptune rules Gemini on VII and Virgo on X; the Saturn transit from a difficult, will-depleting position in the natal opposition with Mars was in the VIIth House; and Pluto was crossing the Midheaven. Her relationship structure was extremely weakened. Her personal perspective was upset. The ego-protection fantasy turned inward. The predisposition could not be held back. The relationship tensions with self and others were critically challenged. These dimensions suggest the possibility of suicide. The break-up of relationship power and success is the beginning of illnesses of all kinds. Suicide, an ultimate illness, defies relationship. We call it "taking life into one's *own* hands."

Life is will. Relationships define perspective.

Conclusion

Throughout this series, the horoscope of Richard Nixon has been studied carefully. The scandal of 1973 through 1974, with its apex in the summer of 1974 has been alluded to often, before the fact. Nixon has had a relationship crisis: with his aides, his oath of office, his country, his frame of reference for personal ambition. He has resigned and, within enormous tensions, he has become dangerously ill. The principal astrological focus of attention, of course, has been the approach of Saturn in transit opposed his Sun in mid-1974 (with other measurements already covered in past volumes and the transit eclipse of the Sun on 20 June 1974 conjunct his extremely important natal Pluto in the Midheaven). Nixon's identity has given in to the relationship pressures, and the worst is yet to come when Saturn conjoins Neptune in opposition to the Sun during the spring and summer of 1975, as the progressed Moon approaches conjunction with natal Saturn.

An analysis of Nixon's illness is very simple, and of course it begins with the tension configuration that dominates his horoscope: Neptune opposed Sun, transited by Saturn. Neptune rules the blood. Saturn rules bloodclots, the congestion, hardening, clogging functions. Phlebitis is an inflammation within the vein, a blood clot formed that can break loose and travel to the heart. Under stress Nixon developed phlebitis. It began in his legs near the knee (Capricorn, Saturn).

Additionally, Nixon's horoscope has the angular X-IV axis tension, involving the Signs Gemini and Sagittarius-Capricorn. His lungs would react under stress (Gemini; pneumonia) as would his legs (Sagittarius, Capricorn).

In *Time* magazine, 30 September 1974, on page 65 an article appeared entitled "Psychosomatic Phlebitis?". The article reported the opinions of Dr. Samuel Silverman, a psychoanalyst and author of *Psychologic Clues in Forecasting Physical Illness,* in relation to Nixon's psychological crisis and phlebitis.

Dr. Silverman is quoted: " 'For years, we've been stuck on the question of whether illness is emotionally or physically caused. It's caused by the interaction, and the clues are psychological as well as physical.' "He is reported further as saying that, when a person develops "critical stress" and cannot cope, either mind or body has to break down. If physical illness strikes, " 'It doesn't do so randomly, but at vulnerable spots unique for each of us.' " He suggests that this uniqueness will depend on which organs have been "sensitized" by heredity, childhood diseases or neurotic strategies. These are the points made by Astrology, precisely.

Purely on the basis of published medical information, Dr. Silverman suggests that Richard Nixon's target areas are " 'the legs (phlebitis in 1964 and 1974, two knee injuries in 1960, foot injury in 1952) and the respiratory system (pneumonia in 1973 and as a child in 1917), with the ominous possibility that the two areas could be connected by a fatal blood clot traveling from leg to lung.' "

That Nixon's introversion keeps his emotions so controlled suggests that the tensions under stress would register in his body. There is reasonable conjecture as well of an instinctive flight into illness (refusing to have his leg bandaged, declining an anticoagulant drug, delay of hospital entrance).

Now pardoned, Nixon is alone with his own conscience, his own time, his own Saturn.

Conclusion

The relationship concept within life—within success, sex, and illness—can not be overemphasized. In all relationships, we are the candles and we are the reflectors. The tensions in life are essential; even the momentary shadows of loss, introspection, and eclipse are vital to the strengthening of self-illumination. The concepts of success, sex, and illness work together to establish whole analysis easily because these dimensions embrace the significances of all other departments of life, the past and the future.

On the day before these pages were written, a young and very attractive woman came for her horoscope analysis. Her horoscope (page 192) shows perfectly the integration of all the concepts studied in this volume. It is a prototypical example, not one selected for any point of extensive corroboration. With the studies of this volume, the following analysis outline is easily possible.

With the Sun in Pisces and the Moon in Scorpio, as well as her Venus conjunct her Mars, her intuitional and sexual levels of expression will require our study. There may ´ be a satirical sense of humor (Sun-Moon blend,

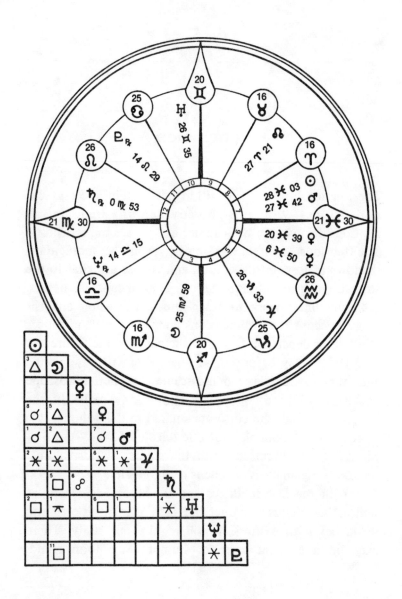

Volume III) and perhaps a strange preoccupation with morbid concerns, death, even the occult, that might cause confusion. At the time of our meeting, she was twenty-five years and seven months old.

Linda is extremely intelligent: the Moon's diurnal motion at birth was 14°02' and in this progressed year is 15°06'; Mercury rules the Midheaven and Ascendant and opposes Saturn. This is the only major opposition within the horoscope. There will be a moodiness and a tendency toward introspection within her intelligence, some limitation, that will have to be worked through in maturity for her to benefit from the potential for wisdom.

Saturn is in Mercury's Sign: her ambition will be to follow painstaking detail and even drudgery to make her point in life. Her intelligence can work very hard. However, the retrogradation suggests a legacy of inferiority feelings, probably taken on in early life from her father. These must be overcome first.

I asked her about her father. Linda said: "he was so exacting; he had polio when I was very young and spent the rest of his life in a respirator. He was a genius, specializing in foreign language interpretation. He was employed by a large company even while confined to the respirator." These facts keyed Uranus within X as the father symbol in Linda's life, and this Uranus is square her Sun and Mars.

It was a simple matter to relate Linda's inferiority feelings to the tension between her and her father (Mercury opposed Saturn, Mercury ruling X; Uranus in X square her Sun, Mars, and Venus). In discussion, she elaborated upon how her father had rigorously tried to train her mind. He taught her to spell technical chemical and engineering words, to understand language concepts while she was just in the early years of school (her Saturn in his third House). He "demanded" that she make something of herself precociously. This depressed her and she eventually rebelled. In studying the transits and progressions of the period of his death when she was fourteen, it was found that her performance in school slumped terribly as soon as he died.

This early tension with her demanding father became extremely important in her life: it affected all her relationships thereafter (Sun and Mars in VII, square Uranus in X). Her relationships with men have been tense and unrewarding. She swore "to give up men" when the progressed Midheaven squared her Neptune in the Ascendant, Neptune ruling Pisces on VII, dispositor of Mercury, Venus, Mars, and the Sun. Within this progressed period, transiting Saturn squared the Sun and Mars, and Linda met a man. After a short-lived affair she became pregnant and had an abortion. That was it.

Saturn rules the Vth and is retrograde in the XIIth. A closer inspection of her sex profile revealed a response anomaly; her only fulfillment was confined to her private fantasy life: Neptune without developmental aspect within the Ascendant (the sextile with Pluto in XI, dispositor of the Moon, ruler of XI, confirms the deduction, corroborated by the native).

Despite all the mental acuity, she was working in a doctor's office in a routine job, secure but "bored silly" (progressed Moon *trine* Uranus at the time of consultation). The Moon is in Scorpio and is in III: Linda is an information go-between. Scorpio keys research. The Virgo Ascendant and the Mercury opposition with Saturn suggest detail and care, stick-to-itiveness. The Sun in VII introduces the public perspective. Mars oriental introduces the promoter. The synthesis portrays Linda as a marketing researcher, a compiler and analyst of details, technical and complicated. With this deduction, she burst out in enthusiasm: "I just *loved* researching papers in college; you're right." And so probably had been her father.

The underachievement in her present job was linked easily with the pressures her father had put upon her early in life. All her relationships were off balance now. She was not being the person she should be. Rebellion and underachievement had become habit.

I suggested that she had become hypercritical as a defense of her rebellion and underachievement (Virgo Ascendant; the Mercury depression reaction when compounded with the nervous development of the Uranus square to the Sun and Mars). She agreed. In her job, she didn't want to meet the challenges her father had placed before her; in her relationships she didn't want to be challenged either, since her relationship difficulties stifled her responses. I even suggested that she fussily "picked fights" with dates toward the end of the evening in order to avoid a challenge to her full-level response: startled, she said that was "absolutely the truth."

This tension in relationships would pile up within the body, of course, and the health profile should reveal it.

Her nails were beautifully manicured, but I suggested that she had a long history of nail-biting (the Uranus square; the Mercury nervousness importance). She said that she had bitten them but had trained herself not to. I asked about her cardiac health, her last electrocardiogram (the Sun conjunct Mars, both squared by Uranus, and the Sun ruling Leo on the XIIth): she said that she had a heart murmur. The Gemini emphasis through Uranus further accurately indicated that she is supersensitive to upper-respiratory ailments.

The Moon in Scorpio is applying to a square with Saturn in XII: there should be a gynecological concern as well. Linda said that she had a cyst on a fallopian tube (Libra's specific rulership of this anatomical zone is involved through the Neptune sextile with Pluto, dispositor of the Moon; Pluto in a separating square with the Moon). The sympathetic relationship between Leo (heart) and Scorpio (gynecological disorder and the abortion) suggested strep throat (Taurus; Venus in square with Uranus); and Linda corroborated a great sensitivity here as well.

The whole analysis hung together: the paternal pressure and the rebellion within relationships; hypercritical self-defenses and therefore a disillusionment with others, with romantic standards; job underachievement; being bored silly.

The whole life was studied through transits and progressions and, through the objectivity established by the horoscope drawing, Linda was able to see the whole syndrome, her difficulties with job success, sexual relationships, and nagging illnesses, without feeling personally threatened. A whole new direction was charted, based upon self-perspective and a kind of willful "turning the switch," to live the life she *could* live. Specifically, Linda's plan was directed toward preparing herself for a research job, to move out of her mother's home, to become her own woman, confident, bright, and deeply knowing, doing what she *needed* to do. Astrologically, the plan was timed with Jupiter's approaching transit of her Sun and Mars in the spring of 1975 (Jupiter natally is in excellent support of Sun, Moon, Venus, and Mars) as Saturn will trine the Sun and Mars from the cusp of the XIth. Linda began to relate better with herself and, therefore, with others. Her candle began to burn more brightly.

This happens time and time again in astrological counseling: lives are adjusted into better light by seeing a self-reflection. Counseling techniques (to be treated in Volume X) focus this light through the objectivity of the horoscope and the astrologer.

It happens time and time again in life: we can surmise how the astrologer pronounced medically dead (page 184) has cherished her life ever since. Through my own critical spine surgery a few years ago (Volume VII), in battle with environmental and personal relationships, I established a new life perspective that has brought grander responsibilities, opportunities, fulfillment and success. The excellent astrologer, Robert Pelletier (*Planets in Aspect*), gained a whole new life perspective and direction through a critical cerebral hemorrhage. Helen Keller, Franklin

Roosevelt, Charles Lindbergh, George Shearing, Ray Charles—all are people who have had to adjust their lives to trauma, who have had to adjust personal perspective and relationships because of critical alteration in their lives.

But why is it that someone apparently in fine relationship with the inner and outer environments *is* incapacitated by business failure, by lovelessness, by illness or death? The will appears strong; success rewards the system; relationships support futher development; yet the identity is critically imbalanced or extinguished. We do not understand why. Perhaps it is here that we approach the limits of Astrology. Perhaps to go beyond this point in conjecture threatens with the sin of *hubris*. Perhaps the astrologer's relationship with God, with the all-pervasive creative principle, must be one of appreciation and reflection—never presumption, pride, or authority. As Martin Buber puts it:

> The perfection of any matter,
> the highest or the lowest,
> touches on the divine.

Appendix

Supplementary Reading List

Success

Luntz, Charles E. *Vocational Guidance by Astrology.*
St. Paul, Minnesota: Llewellyn Publications, 1969.

Sex

May, Rollo. *Love and Will.* New York: Dell
Publishing Company, 1969.
Robson, Vivian E. *Astrology and Human Sex Life.*
Hackensack, New Jersey: Wheman Bros., 1963.

Synastry

Burroughs, Melba. *Life & Love.* St. Paul, Minnesota:
Llewellyn Publications, 1973.
Rodden, Lois M. *The Mercury Method of Chart
Comparison.* Hollywood, California: 1973.

Illness

Cornell, H. L. *Encyclopaedia of Medical Astrology.*
St. Paul, Minnesota: Llewellyn Publications, 1972.
Doane, Doris Chase. *Astrology: 30 Years Research.*
Los Angeles.
Garrison, Omar V. *Medical Astrology.* New Hyde Park,
New York: University Books, Inc., 1971.

General

Tyl, Noel. *The Horoscope as Identity.* St. Paul,
Minnesota: Llewellyn Publications, 1974.

These books may be obtained through your local bookdealer or through Llewellyn Publications, Box 3383, St. Paul, Minnesota 55165.

The Principles and Practice of Astrology
for home study and college curriculum
by Noel Tyl
in twelve volumes

I. Horoscope Construction

Here is an unrivaled explanation of the construction of a horoscope. All time and position corrections are made maximally clear. A totally self-contained volume, with tables and practice horoscope blanks. Contents include: calculating the time of birth—step-by-step guidance, use of materials and examples; measuring the houses—what they are, how they're placed; the calligraphy—the symbols of astrology, meaning of the signs, illustrative birthdays of famous people; placing the planets—measuring planetary movement, test horoscopes; calculation review—special time problems explained; the Sun and the signs—the Sun as the key, Sun Sign interpretations, the elements, polarities, modes; the ruling planets—meaning and function of planets in the chart with sample horoscopes reviewed; the Age of Aquarius—what it is and what it means to astrologers.

II. The Houses: Their Signs and Planets

The rationale of house demarcation, the meanings of the signs upon each house, the planets' significance in every house; derivative house readings.

III. The Planets: Their Signs and Aspects

A full expansion of the elements and modes in a refreshingly modern style; the significance of every planet within every sign; the reading of aspects and dignities "at a glance"; the suggested meanings of all major aspects and Sun-Moon combinations. An invaluable master reference book for horoscope interpretation.

IV. Aspects and Houses in Analysis

Analytical synthesis technique presented through many examples, showing hemisphere emphasis, retrogradation patterns, the grand trine, the grand square, the T square in complete explanation, the lunar nodal axis, parallels of declination, and the part of fortune; the "law of naturalness." A volume devoted totally to the art of synthesis.

V. Astrology and Personality

Never before presented: an explanation of psychological theories of personality translated into astrological terms and technique! The theories of Kurt Lewin, Carl Jung, Henry Murray, Abraham Maslow, Erich Fromm, Alfred Adler and Sigmund Freud; and astrological glossary of psychological terms and personality traits.

VI. The Expanded Present

An introduction to prediction, an analysis of the time dimension in astrology; application and separation of aspects, "rapport" measurements, secondary progression, primary directions, "factor 7" analysis. Many examples clarify the work of astrology toward understanding change and development in personality, within free-will and fate.

VII. Integrated Transits

A definitive work, modernizing the rationale, analysis and application of transit theory, in accord with the needs and expectations of modern people. Astrology is translated into behavior with many real-life examples for every major transit. The work also includes studies of solar revolution, rectification, eclipse theory, and accidents.

VIII. Analysis and Prediction

A gallery of astrological portraits: the whole-view of astrological analysis; inspection of the past, expansion of the present, the creation of the future. Each step of deduction, analysis, and projection is presented in the sharing of real-life horoscopes: *you* become the astrologer! Radix methods, progressions, and transits are fully interpreted. In addition, there is an introduction to Horary and Electional Astrology.

IX. Special Horoscope Dimensions

Success: vocation, relocation, opportunity, elections. Sex: chart comparison, sex profile, love, homosexuality, abortion, creativity. Illness: health problems, surgery, vitality.

X. Astrological Counsel

Never before presented: a full, detailed inspection of the psychodynamics of the astrologer-client relationship, with examples showing the astrologer's consideration of the horoscope *and* the individual, bringing together the personality and its time structure for fulfillment. Difficulties analyzed, communication techniques explored.

XI. Astrology: Astral, Mundane, Occult

The fixed stars, the individual degrees and decanates; considerations of mundane astrology governing international events; study of death and reincarnation, the areas shared by astrology and occult studies.

XII. Times to Come

A projection of astrology into the future, investigating the potential of astrology. A complete subject index for all twelve volumes.

Teacher's Guide

Not part of the series, but for educators teaching astrology. A complete explanation of all subjects: difficulties, suggested techniques, test examinations for each step of development.

The Horoscope as Identity   **Price $10.00**

Studies in the Astrology of Sex, Ambition, and Identity within modern, freer times.   **by Noel Tyl**

What the publisher says:

If this is truly a New Age that we have entered, the Age of Aquarius, then there must be new things said: new interpretations of the Ancient Wisdom of which we are the guardians.

At Llewellyn we receive an average of one manuscript every day—most of them saying nothing, some of them saying old things in new ways, some of them publishable. For a cycle of twelve years I waited to see a manuscript that said something new in astrology—and I waited in vain. I did not see a single astrological book meeting that ideal until the exact completion of that twelve-year cycle in February of 1973—and then it happened!

As far as Llewellyn is concerned, a new star was born on the day that I completed reading the manuscript of *The Horoscope as Identity*.

The author of this book actually incarnates the new influx of psychological meaning in terms of astrological practice that this Age demands. He speaks to the needs of the present and coming student of astrology and psychology combined as they should be.

This is not a book of tables, or a repetition of what is said well or poorly in so many other books. It is not a book that sees astrology as frozen in medieval times and meanings. It is a book for both the advanced student of astrology and the intelligent layman who wants to see what is really in modern astrology. It is a book for the reader who is ready to be liberated—who will be able to use the knowledge of self and this world to achieve freedom and mastery of his destiny that is the goal of all astrological and psychological analysis.

The particular value of this book is the modern understanding of Saturn in the chart, the concept of the sex-profile, and the guidance to speed-reading the horoscope. Case studies include: Albert Speer, Hitler's architect; a famous businessman (survival or death); Judy Garland.

Fifty-eight horoscope charts illustrate the text.

These books are available through Llewellyn Publications (Box 3383, St. Paul, Minnesota 55165) or through your local bookdealer.

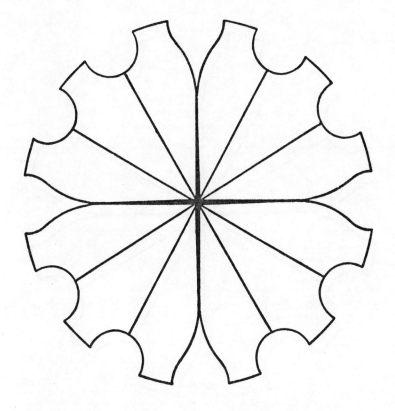

Small blanks for practice only; large-circle form
recommended. Order recommended blanks, style 9 (with
aspect grid), package of 100, AS5-$3.00, from Llewellyn
Publications, Box 3383, St. Paul, Minnesota 55165, or from
your local bookdealer. Other astrological tools, such as
Ephemerides, etc., may be obtained there also.

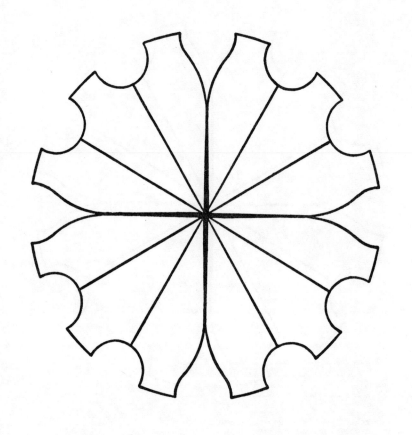

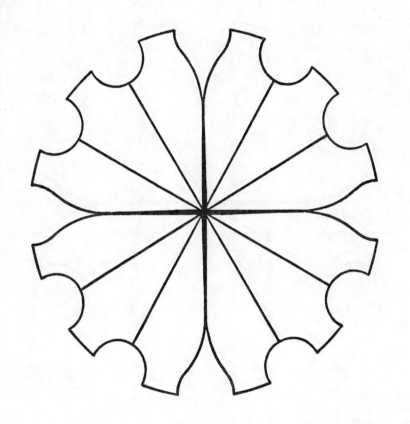

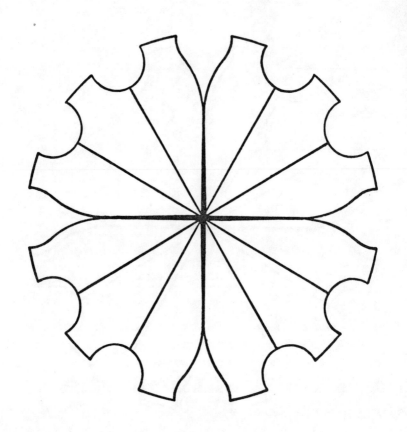

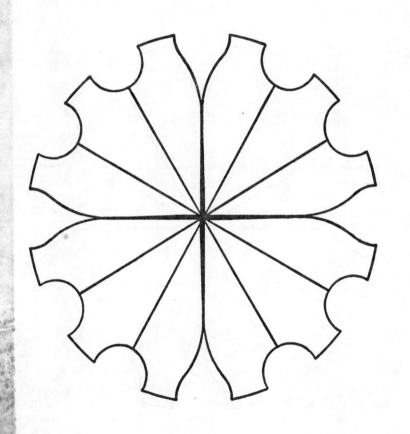